Ladder on the Fence

MARGARET LYGNOS

Ladder on the Fence
© Margaret Lygnos, 2022
First published 2022

ISBN 978-0-9944362-5-2

Production by PB Publishing
Gisborne Victoria Australia
www.pbublishing.com.au

Cover design: Jennifer Snape Graphic Design

All rights reserved. Without limiting the rights under copyright as reserved, no part of this publication may be reproduced, stored in or introduced into a database and retrieval system or transmitted in any form or any means (electronic, mechanical, photocopying, recording or otherwise) without the prior written permission of the author.
Author's email: minasmarg@hotmail.com

Printed by IngramSpark Australia

NATIONAL
LIBRARY
OF AUSTRALIA

Contents

	Introduction	1
1	Doll's House	3
2	Television	6
3	Bob	10
4	We Find Bob	26
5	Tommy	30
6	The Red Traffic Light	34
7	Fun In The Garden	41
8	Sunday School	46
9	The Street Where We Lived	60
10	Kindergarten	69
11	School 1	70
12	Bayswater	77
13	School 2	79
14	Christmas and Birthdays	83
15	The City	86
16	Horse and Cart	89
17	Cousins	92

18	Dreams	98
19	Grade Four	100
20	The School Fete	102
21	Gerry The Dog	103
22	Andrew	104
23	Fires	107
24	Those Pants	109
25	Out At Night	111
26	Valentines	114
27	More School	117
28	Vanity	120
29	Mum's Traditional Cooking	121
30	Male Anatomy	124
31	Gaffney Street	128
32	More School	130
33	The Beatles	135
34	Peeping Tom	137
35	Losing My Religion	138
36	Transport And Tossers Or Why I Stopped Using Public Transport	143
37	My Future	145
	Epilogue	146

Introduction

Ladder on the Fence is a collection of memories from my childhood. Each chapter has been written as I remembered the events so sometimes the stories are not in chronological order. The events are true as I remember them or as I remember them being told to me.

I am a Baby Boomer. I was born in January 1947, a post war baby, the second in a family of four children, three of whom were boys. My parents met during the war years and, as my father was in the Air Force stationed somewhere in the north of Australia, they did not see each other very often: not until the end of the war when they were married. During their time apart, my mother worked in an office for the only time in her life.

We lived a comfortable life in Moonee Ponds in a house which had belonged to my father's parents. The house was left to my father and his brother, Bob. Dad bought Bob's share of the house and that's where my childhood was spent and where my mother spent fifty-four of her ninety-eight years. My mother was thirty-eight when she married and my father was forty.

My father was an aircraft mechanic working at Essendon Airport, also known as the Essendon Aerodrome. He rode his pushbike to the 'Drome each morning (that's what he called it) and it was on this well-travelled ride that he was killed. He was run over by a large truck from a local quarry company and never regained consciousness. It was at this point that my life took an obvious unhappy turn and a once-comfortable life became uncomfortable.

Some of these memories were written a long time ago and some more recently.

Doll's House

When I was three or four years old, my father made me a doll's house. He had been working secretly in his shed on the toy house, which was made from a pattern bought from a Melbourne newspaper. When it was given to me, I was thrilled beyond words. What little girl wouldn't like a doll's house full of small pieces of furniture and little dolls? My father had made two little wooden beds and a three-piece lounge suite and my mother had dressed the dolls and made bed covers. There was a staircase leading up to two rooms on the upper floor. The front and back walls came off and one side of the roof lifted up allowing access to the rooms upstairs. Dad had even fitted tiny hinges on the back door. The house was on castors and I could wheel it all over the house or on to the front veranda to play. I played endlessly with my doll's house and sometimes I would pretend I could go inside and live in it with my little dolls.

I still have the doll's house. My children enjoyed playing with it and now my grandchildren have fun and enjoy it. I don't have many memories of my father but the one about the doll's house is vivid.

One day he took my older brother and me on a tram to Essendon Airport so we could see where he worked. He seemed to be very proud of us and showed us all over the hangar where the huge aeroplanes were parked during maintenance and repair work.

We were able to go into one of the planes he had been working on and into the cockpit where we sat in the pilot's seat watching one of his colleagues work. We didn't catch the tram home but walked all the way because he told us we could have a special ice-cream if we walked. Naturally we agreed and were rewarded with an ice-cream cone covered in chocolate and dipped in hundreds and thousands. I had never seen such a delicacy.

Another time, Dad took my older brother and me on a chartered flight for family members of the workers just to see the lights of Melbourne at night. It was a beautiful, spectacular sight, like circling over a scene in fairyland.

I remember watching Dad put bicycle clips on the cuffs of his trousers before riding off to do a night shift, and I remember him catching a mouse in the pantry and carrying it outside by the tail. He painted a little room for me with pale green paint and he and Mum surprised me by making it my bedroom. I had a new pink bedspread and white curtains and my very own white dressing table with an oval mirror. Beside my bed there was a little cupboard which was also painted white and I kept my books in there. I gave that dear little cupboard to my daughter for her daughter and she keeps books in it now too.

One thing my brothers and I had was plenty of books. My mother's family were an artistic bunch, artists and writers. Mum read to us frequently, not only at night but also during the day. We had AA Milne, Beatrix Potter, Charles Kingsley, Rudyard Kipling, etc, etc. Lots of books. Mum was a member of a library in Puckle Street where, for a small fee, she would borrow books for herself and for us. I remember a book called Sammy the Silverfish and another called The Muggles of Mugwumpier, not books that are read today and actually, I have never heard of them again.

My dad shaved with a safety razor each day and, before applying it to his face, he sharpened it on a leather strap which hung in the bathroom. After work he always had a shower and rubbed barrier cream into his hands. He rolled his own cigarettes but he didn't smoke much. He drank beer but only occasionally. He liked to sit on a cane chair in the kitchen and read the paper after work. One day, when Dad was sitting in the kitchen in his comfortable chair reading a magazine before dinner, I saw a picture of a television set on the back page. He said he would probably buy one for us when they came to Australia. He never got to see a television because he died in 1954. Television didn't arrive in Australia until 1956.

Dad sometimes teased my mother because she was always running late or had burnt another saucepan or had forgotten to put salt in the meatballs. On weekends we often went to Elwood to see Grandma and Grandpa, Mum's parents. The trip involved two trains and a tram ride and took about an hour and a half if everything was on time. On one particular day, Mum was not ready and Dad got sick of waiting, so he said we would start walking and meet her at Moonee Ponds train station. My older brother and I walked with Dad to the station where he bought our tickets. We let one train go but when the next one came along Dad said we should get on it. About an hour or so after we arrived at our grandparents' home, Mum arrived. She was really mad at Dad but he thought it was funny and teased her about always being late. She wouldn't talk to him for several days. Having four children, Mum probably had heaps to do before she could go out of the house so she was always running late.

Television

In 1956, the Olympic Games came to Melbourne and so did television. Our local church bought a television so that the church members could watch the games. Mum said I could go and have a look one night, as long as my older brother kept an eye on me. He said he would but as soon as we shut the gate behind us, he tore off down the hill, around the corner and into the church grounds. I followed, trying to keep up, but couldn't. I got there safely, but no thanks to him.

My first memory of television is a small glass-fronted box with fuzzy black and white pictures of people running very fast from one side to the other. I couldn't see anything very clearly because the front seats were occupied by large bodies who yelled in a way I had never seen or heard before. It didn't seem very interesting to me so I went outside to play on the church steps with my friend. There were two wooden staircases at the side entrances to the church where all the girls liked to play house and the boys played ships. We played until some bigger girls came and pushed us off the stairs so we had to find somewhere else to play. We sat on the swings in the dark while I waited for my brother to walk home with me, but he was nowhere to be seen. Eventually I ran home in the dark, squealing at every shadow that moved. On reaching home, my brother was waiting for me in the front garden with his friend. They were smoking cigarettes.

"Why didn't you wait for me at the church," I asked.

He pulled a face at me and tried to blow a smoke ring but began to cough so much that I thought he was going to choke.

"Do you want me to get Mum?" I asked him.

"No, idiot," he said.

"You shouldn't smoke. Mum won't like you smoking."

"Mum won't know if you don't tell, and you better not or I'll tell on you."

"What for?" I asked.

"I know it was you who ate all the sugared orange peel," he smirked.

I don't know how he knew, but it was true—I had eaten a large amount of the delicious peel and paid for it with a tummy ache and the runs.

When we ate oranges Mum would keep all the peel then boil it and cut it into narrow strips before rolling it in sugar. It was like eating lollies and we didn't have lollies very often. Still, I didn't eat that much again. At least I tried not to.

We went inside and Mum asked us about the television.

"Boring," I said.

"Great," said my brother.

"Bed," said Mum.

We didn't have a television because they were quite expensive and we were not well off after Dad died. When we walked around the neighbourhood it was easy to see who had a television because you needed a huge antenna on the roof, which was a dead giveaway. Sometimes we were surprised to see who could afford a television and who, like us, could not.

Mum would say, "They have a television yet they can't even weed their garden," or "Wouldn't you think they would paint their house before buying a television?"

Mum was funny like that.

We had to make do with listening to the radio or reading books, which wasn't that bad really. We sat in the kitchen in front of the wood fire stove where it was really warm, and we toasted bread on top of the hotplates. When it was very cold, we took turns to put our feet in the open oven after Mum had cooked the dinner, and she often hung wet socks over the oven door to dry.

On the radio, there were serials like Dad and Dave, Biggles, When a Girl Marries and Blue Hills to name a few, and there were also programs just for children like The Argonauts. On Saturday mornings there was a talent quest called The Three Gongs, where only the very best singers or musicians got three gongs. It was okay because we didn't know what it was like to have a television. Besides, you could do more than one thing when listening to the radio, such as colouring in, feeding the cat or even peeling potatoes.

In the local shopping strip called Puckle Street, there were all types of shops including an electrical goods store. To get people interested in buying a television set, the shop had one turned on and visible in the window all the time. Heaps of people stood three deep watching whatever was on, even though there was no sound and you had to guess what the people on the screen were saying. When I look back now, it seems so silly but it was just so amazing to us.

Our next-door neighbours, who were not poor like us, bought a television and put it in their sitting room. Their sitting room window was about a metre and a half from our adjoining fence and one of my brothers somehow discovered the TV set and alerted us. We tried jumping up and hanging on to the top of the fence but that hurt our hands, so we dragged kitchen chairs out to the fence but they were not high enough. Besides, Mum yelled at us to "Bring those chairs inside you wretched children!"

Then my older brother remembered two small ladders that were up on the rafters in the shed. He climbed on the workbench and pulled the ladders down and we rushed them over to the fence. At last we could see the television, over the fence, through the lace curtains and three metres from the window. It was a black and white picture. That's all I know. There were three of us and two ladders and someone was always falling off and yelling. Our neighbours heard us and pulled the blind down.

The next day Mum said, "What are those ladders doing on the fence?"

No one answered. She said, "Put them away, and don't be such stickybeaks."

We put them away after a few more attempts at watching because we could not see anything worthwhile. The people who lived there were very kind to us and sometimes they invited us in to watch something special. They also took phone messages for Mum from her parents, who lived in Elwood. I remember the day she returned from next door crying quietly, having been told her mother had died. I had arranged to go to the beach with other neighbours and was very annoyed when Mum told me I couldn't go.

"How can you think of going to the beach when your grandmother has just died?" she said to me.

When I look back, I know that was insensitive but I had been taught to ignore feelings and to soldier on no matter what.

Bob

Uncle Bob was my father's only brother—both had a pretty difficult life. My father managed to make a success of his life, unlike poor Uncle Bob who had suffered from depression and a lack of confidence from early childhood. After spending some time in an asylum, he came to see my father to talk over his future.

My mother did not like Bob and although it happened over sixty years ago, I remember the conversation and events as if it happened yesterday.

"No, Mack. I don't want him in the house," said Mum.

"Ah, come on Ede!" said Dad.

"No. He's weird and I don't like or trust the blighter."

"But he's had a really hard time," said Dad.

"I don't care. He should be back in that lunatic asylum."

These words coloured my image of Uncle Bob, my father's only brother, so when I first saw him, I was amazed at his ordinary appearance. I had expected a hunch-backed, crazy-eyed, Enid Blyton type of villain. Instead, he looked a lot like my father. He kept his head lowered to avoid eye contact, his clothes were a bit grubby and he shuffled his feet. But through the eyes of a six-year-old girl, he looked okay. In retrospect, I know he was a tortured soul.

"Margaret, this is your Uncle Bob," said Dad. We were outside in Dad's workshop.

"Hello," I replied quietly.

Uncle Bob smiled at me but I don't remember him saying anything directly to me.

"This is for the girl," he said, handing a medium-sized cardboard box to my father. Dad shook the box gently before giving it to me.

"Go and ask your mother to put the kettle on," Dad said, giving me a gentle nudge and a chance to run away and open the box in private.

"Mum, Mum, Uncle Bob brought me a present," I yelled, bursting into the kitchen.

"Hmm," said Mum. "Well, aren't you going to open it?"

Kneeling at the kitchen table where Mum was preparing afternoon tea, I opened the box.

"It's a clock, Mum. Look."

"Hmm, alarm clock. Probably doesn't work," said Mum.

I fiddled with the clock. I wound it and found that it began to tick.

"It does work. See?" I said.

"Does your father want a cup of tea yet?"

"Yes, he does." I had almost forgotten.

I sat outside on the top step with my clock. My brothers wanted to play with it but I wouldn't let them. It wasn't every day I got a present like this. Through the wire door I could hear Dad and Uncle Bob yarning at the kitchen table. Mum busied herself away from them, keeping herself aloof, her displeasure obvious.

"Why don't you go up north for a bit of a holiday?" Dad suggested.

"Ya. Reckon I should."

"Yes," said Dad.

"Cost a lot though," grumbled Uncle Bob.

"You've got plenty of money since we bought your half of this house."

"Yeah. Maybe I'll look into a trip," Uncle Bob said quietly.

I whizzed the hands of the clock around and around. That night at bedtime, Dad tried to set the alarm for me but it would not work.

About a month later, Uncle Bob appeared again. Careful to avoid my mother, he came around to Dad's workshop where I was helping him as he mended our shoes. I handed him the tacks that held the metal tips in place on the heels and toes of the shoes.

"G'day Bob. Thought you must have gone up north by now," Dad said.

"Just on my way. Came to say goodbye. Might not see you for some time," Bob replied.

"Going on the bus, are you?" asked Dad.

"No."

"Train?"

"No."

"Flying?"

"No."

"Well, how the hell are you going?" Dad asked.

"Bought a horse and cart. Ten quid the lot."

"What?" yelled Dad. "That'll take forever."

"Yeah, well I reckon I've got plenty of time."

"Suppose you have," Dad replied.

"I'll be off then," said Uncle Bob, beginning to walk away.

I ran around to the front gate with the two men. I wanted to see the horse. She was an old grey mare with a dusty coat and a tangled mane. Her eyes were barely open and her head hung so low her nose almost touched the ground. She was hitched to a small open cart, the colour of an old paling fence. Grey horse, grey cart. Dad and Uncle Bob stood at the curb.

"Looks a bit old Bob, don't you think?" Dad said, as he rubbed his chin.

"No, she's okay. The chap I bought her from says she's got plenty of life in her yet."

"I've seen healthier horses at the glue factory." Dad sounded concerned.

Bob climbed up into the cart and grabbed the reins.

"Giddy-up there," he said.

The horse opened its tired, old eyes.

"Move on." Uncle Bob flicked the reins.

The horse shuddered and stumbled forward. Then, with enormous effort, the poor old thing began to pull the cart slowly up the hill towards the main road.

"Come inside and leave that old fool alone," Mum called from the front door. "Your dinner is ready."

We washed our hands and sat down to eat. We had barely taken a mouthful when we heard a commotion outside in the street. Next, there was a loud banging at the front door.

"Mack? Mack, are you there?" called our neighbour. "It's your brother Bob. He's in a spot of bother."

Dad hurried outside and we all followed. Even Mum came.

"What's happened to the poor bastard now?" I heard Dad saying, as he hurried up the street to where a small crowd had gathered.

In a loud excited voice, the neighbour replied, "Bob had the horse and cart pulled up at the main road waiting to cross to the other side. A car roared past and backfired—it was like a gunshot. The poor horse got such a fright; it bolted straight across the intersection. The horse and cart were almost hit by another car. When they reached the other side of the road, the horse dropped dead."

There was poor Uncle Bob standing beside the cart looking at the unfortunate horse lying at his feet.

"At least we won't have to shoot the poor thing," said Dad.

We did not see Uncle Bob for a long time after that, but we did not forget him in a hurry. Dad must have worried about him because he often said, "Wonder what poor old Bob's up to?" or, "That brother of mine could be dead and we would never know."

Sometimes, my brothers and I would ask Dad to tell us stories about Uncle Bob because they were entertaining and funny.

"Tell us the one about the shirts, Dad."

That was the one I liked best.

"You want to hear that one again?" Dad laughed.

"Yes, yes," we chorused.

"Well," Dad began, "we were working on a farm just out of Bendigo."

"Did you ride horses on the farm, Dad?" I asked.

"Yes we rode horses and on Sunday we rode over to Aunt Hilda's house for lunch," he said.

"Did you go every week?" I asked.

"Just about. She said we were welcome as long as we wore a collar and tie and no hob-nailed boots in the house."

"Come on Dad. Tell us about Bob's shirts," I said.

"Bob always had three shirts."

"What colour were they?"

"I can't remember. Probably blue or white. It was hard to tell because they were always dirty," said Dad.

"Why were they dirty, Dad?" one of us would ask.

These questions were necessary even though we knew the answers. We just wanted to keep Dad on track.

Dad continued, "Well, he didn't believe in washing his clothes, seemed to think it was a waste of time. He wore them till they were very dirty, then he would give them to the dogs to sleep on and buy three new ones. Each Sunday morning, before going to see Aunt Hilda, he would get out his three dirty shirts, lay them out on his bed and choose the cleanest one."

"Did he ask you to help him choose?" my brother asked.

"No. He would look at them all very carefully and decide which was the cleanest and that's the one he wore."

"Did he smell, Dad?"

"Well, I don't know about that but Aunt Hilda said to him one Sunday that if he did not have a clean shirt to wear next week, he needn't bother coming."

"So, what did he do, Dad? Tell us what he did," we begged.

"I'm not sure why, but this time he decided to wash his shirts," said Dad.

"How did he do it? How did he wash his shirts, Dad?" asked one of my brothers, laughing with excitement.

"Well, he got a large hessian sack, put in a couple of bars of soap, threw in his dirty shirts and tied up the bag with a piece of rope. He tied the rope to a tree and chucked the bag into the river for a few days."

"Did that clean his shirts, Dad?" I asked.

"It must have, because Aunt Hilda gave him lunch on Sundays and he didn't have to throw out those shirts for a couple more months.

My Dad loved to tell us stories and one winter afternoon as we sat around the fire listening to the radio, he told us a very sad story.

POOR OLD BOB, as told by my father.

"Aunt Hilda," he said, "wasn't really my aunt. She was a cousin who was like a mother to Bob and me when we were little tackers. She looked after us until we were old enough to go to school. You see, Bob and I were born in Hong Kong in nineteen hundred and six and nineteen hundred and seven."

"Was your father a Chinaman, Dad?"

"No," laughed Dad. "My father was from Scotland and we lived in Hong Kong because of his work. He was the captain of a merchant ship called the Hungshang. Our mother lived a very carefree social life. She had many friends and we hardly ever saw her. We had servants in the home and ayahs, women who cared for Bob and me from birth. Both of us were unwell for a long time so our mother took us to see a well-respected English doctor in Hong Kong.

"Well, Mrs Mack," said the doctor, "it's clear to me these two boys of yours are not thriving in the Hong Kong environment."

"But doctor, they are well cared for and given everything they need. They have always had two women looking after them," said my mother.

"Perhaps they need only one woman to look after them," said the doctor.

"What do you mean?"

"I mean, they probably need their mother. My advice to you, Mrs Mack, is to take the two boys home to Australia, to a better climate and a different life."

My mother hated her new life in Australia and resented the separation from her social life and her husband because she only saw him twice a year. Once we were settled in Australia, it became obvious that my mother was not interested in looking after Bob and me. She spent a lot of time giving and attending afternoon tea parties to make friends with the local families. We were neglected and our health did not improve much. Luckily for us, Aunt Beatrice, Mother's older sister, came to visit us.

"These two boys of yours look half-starved," said Aunt Beatrice to my mother.

"Well, I don't seem to be able to provide the sort of food they like."

"They are also very grubby. Their hair hasn't been washed in weeks!"

"I'm not really cut out for motherhood," Mum replied.

"That's obvious. Perhaps they should come and live with me for a while and I'll fatten them up," said Aunt Beatrice.

She took the two of us up to Ballarat to live with her family of ten children. When we arrived, her husband shook his head in disbelief.

"For God's sake Bee! Haven't we got enough mouths to feed already?"

"Don't worry. I've got it all worked out," said Aunt Beatrice, as she walked to the back door and pulled it open.

"Hil—da!" she yelled at the top of her voice.

A tall, fair-headed girl with brown eyes smiled at us as she appeared from around the side of the house.

"Hello Mum. What have you got here?" said Hilda, giving her mother a hug.

"These two little ragamuffins are your cousins. They are going to stay with us for a while and you can take care of them."

Hilda was given sole responsibility for the two of us. She took us under her wing and did the best a sixteen-year-old could do with two frightened little boys. She shared her bed with us, our short skinny legs at one end kicking Hilda's long legs at the other. Sometimes she would wake to find her feet in a puddle but she was never cross with us.

"Come on you two little wet-a-beds, help me drag this wet mattress out into the sunshine."

She taught us nursery rhymes, which the three of us sang together loudly as we worked. When the work was done, we went outside to play. We ran in the sunshine, we rolled in the grass and we climbed trees. It seemed like endless hours of happiness and laughter.

At bedtime we cuddled up to Hilda waiting for a story. Her stories were new and exciting to us so we fought off sleep, always determined to hear the end. We adored her and were never far from her side. Sadly, those happy days did not last for long.

One day, Hilda said, "I've got something special to tell you both so I'm taking you into the fern gully for a picnic."

We ate our lunch beside a stream and then lay back in the grass to listen to the bush. Cockatoos and corellas screeched overhead and bees buzzed in the gum blossoms nearby. Everything about that afternoon is clearly imprinted in my mind because of what she told us next.

"Come and sit close to me," she said, putting an arm around each of us.

"What do you want to tell us?" we asked.

"It's time for you two to go back and live with your mother," she said. "You are both old enough to start school now and your mother wants you back."

For the second time in our short lives, we were torn away from our little bit of love and security and taken back to Melbourne by train. It was 1912. We only returned to Ballarat after that for school holidays.

Physically we thrived but emotionally we suffered badly. When we cried there was no one to dry our tears, no one to cuddle us, so we learnt not to cry. There was no point. Poor Bob suffered more than I and was always trying to get our mother's attention and approval, but she took very little notice of him.

"Mother, I can read now," said Bob, holding up his school reader.

"Yes, well so you should," said our mother, never bothering to stop and listen to her son read.

"Mother, I can run really fast," Bob would say.

"Well you shouldn't run. You will fall over and hurt yourself."

"Mother, look at my drawing of father's ship."

"Don't be silly, that's nothing like your father's ship," she would reply.

"Mother, I don't feel well."

"Don't bother me now. I'm going out."

"But my head aches badly."

"Get off to school."

Poor Bob. When he was unwell he sometimes hid in the stables where he could rest all day. Once I found him on the way home from school. He was asleep under a tree in the park. He had been sent to school but, feeling sick, was too weak to make it.

I coped better and when I finished primary school, I was awarded a certificate for perfect attendance. How could any child possibly be well enough to attend school on every school day for seven years? My mother was a very hardhearted woman.

As soon as I was old enough, I left home, leaving the office job my mother had insisted I try. I headed for Ballarat and did any type of work I could find on the land and in the town. I became a Jack-of-all-trades. Bob stayed with Mother, always trying to make her happy but never succeeding. He was very unhappy with the work my mother found for him at the bank. Finally, through Father's connections, he obtained work on board a ship. Poor old Bob, always unlucky, became unwell as they sailed through Bass Strait and was taken off the ship and admitted to hospital in Fremantle.

Bob woke after an operation to remove his appendix and found himself looking up into the pretty face of a nurse, Mary Andrews. She knew he was a long way from home and was very kind to him. After his discharge from hospital, they kept in touch. He had no work and not much money. Mary's father owned an ice works and she persuaded him to give Bob a job. He worked as an iceman, delivering ice during the day and filling ice chests that people used to keep their food cool in those days. That was before fridges. Mary's father took pity on Bob at Christmas and took him home to spend the day with his family. As he ate his Christmas pudding, Bob looked up at pretty Mary seated opposite him, pulled a threepenny piece which he had just bitten from his mouth, and fell in love. The young woman was equally smitten and so began a secret love affair. For the first time in Bob's life, he loved someone who loved him in return.

Bob approached Mary's father hoping to have his permission to marry Mary.

"Mr Andrews sir? Can I speak with you please?"

"Yes, Bob. What can I do for you, my boy?" said Mr Andrews.

"Well your daughter, Mary and I…"

"What have you to do with my daughter?" said Mr Andrews, his voice rising.

"Well, we have become good friends you know." Bob stopped because he could already sense that things were not going well.

"Friends are all you will ever be Bob. You don't have two pennies to rub together. You can't hope for the likes of Mary. Come back and ask me when you're in a better financial position and not before."

Mary cried when Bob told her, "But Bob, we have to get married, I'm going to have a baby."

Bob didn't know whether to be happy or sad. It was true, he had very little money and only now could he see the necessity of having it.

"I know what to do. I'll go home and ask Mother for help," said Bob.

"Let me come with you to meet her," Mary cried. "I have some money to help with the fares."

"Yes," agreed Bob, who could not bear to be separated from Mary.

They left without telling Mary's parents and several days later, boarded a ship for Melbourne. They arrived in Port Melbourne early one morning and caught the train straight to Moonee Ponds to see our mother.

"You wait outside, Mary, and I'll go inside and tell her," Bob suggested.

"Don't be too long, will you."

Mother was very surprised to see Bob and was even more surprised to hear that he wanted to get married immediately and that he wanted money.

"Well I'm glad that you have met someone to marry but you will have to wait until you have worked a little longer and saved some money," she advised.

"But we don't want to wait. We want to be married as soon as possible," Bob replied.

"Bob, I will not give you my money. You have to learn to stand on your own two feet. Just work hard for a year or two. Then you can think about getting married."

"We can't wait a year or two, we have to get married," said Bob.

"Why do you have to get married? Bob, what have you been up to?" asked Mother.

"We love each other Mother. When you meet her, you will love her too," pleaded Bob.

"I won't love her and I do not wish to meet such a girl."

"She's outside, Mother. She's waiting to meet you."

Mother walked to the front door and saw Mary standing outside on the veranda. She seemed to change her mind.

"Let me speak to her. Bring her inside and leave us alone for a while."

Bob brought Mary into the house, his face beaming with delight.

"Mother, this is Mary Andrews," said Bob.

"Leave us a while, Bob. Let us talk alone. Go down the hill and see Bill. He's been asking after you for months."

Bob went off happily to see his old friend and returned an hour later to have all of his happiness ruined by mother's explanation of what had happened.

"She's gone Bob. She was no good; fancy you bringing a girl like that here. She won't be back to bother you and you don't have to marry her now," explained Mother.

"But I want to marry her! I love her. She loves me."

"I gave her enough money to get home and she was happy to take it and go."

"I'll go after her. And I'm never coming back," said Bob.

Bob rushed into his room to pick up his bag and Mother rushed after him. All the windows in the old house were barred and the solid doors all had large keys permanently in the locks. She shut the door, turned the key and poor Bob was imprisoned by our mother, who had been given a chance to redeem herself but failed dreadfully. Bob wailed and banged on the door but Mother refused to speak to him.

Poor Bob. He nearly went mad, and I only found out about him because one of the neighbours wrote me a letter.

'Dear Mack,   February 1930

There's a bit of trouble at home with Bob. He seems to be spending a bit of time camped up on the roof. Not sure what has happened but Bob seems to be very upset. His hair has grown very long and sometimes he moans and yells for hours on end, usually at night. Your mother refuses to open the door when I knock. I think you had better come home.

Your old friend, Bill.'

Dad stopped his storytelling, visibly upset.

"Was he really living on the roof, Dad?" we asked.

"Yes. Bob was indeed living up on the roof. He had managed to get into the ceiling by standing on top of the wardrobe in his room then he climbed through a manhole. He'd removed some slates and climbed onto the roof where he made a campsite. He'd tied a rope between two chimneys and thrown a quilt over it to make a little tent. It's a big house and there's enough room up there on the roof for half a dozen people to live. Mother was leaving food for him in his room. Bob only went inside the house to get things he needed. He was so heartbroken. He cried like a baby when I climbed up onto the roof to see him. He fell into my arms and sobbed. I was the only person he would speak to and he told me everything that had happened. I tried to help. I wrote a letter to Mr Andrews and received an answer within a month.

'Dear Mr Mack,

I am sorry to tell you that neither my daughter Mary nor I have ever known a man by the name of Bob Mack, he must have been mistaken. My daughter Mary has been married these past few months to an old family friend and is expecting a little one very soon.

Yours sincerely   **Duncan Andrews'**

About a year after the horse and cart incident, my father was killed in an accident riding his bike to work at the Essendon Airport. Bob arrived the day after the funeral. They couldn't wait for Bob so he missed his only brother's funeral. My brothers and I missed our father's funeral also. Not because we were not there but because we were only children and the family thought we shouldn't be involved. I think they didn't think.

I stood in my room miserable and alone. I heard a familiar sound in the backyard. Someone was chopping wood.

"It must be Dad," I yelled. "Dad chops the wood."

I ran out into the yard calling at the top of my voice, "Dad's back. He's outside chopping wood. It's all a mistake."

But I'd made the mistake. It wasn't Dad, but Uncle Bob.

He stayed for an hour or so and chopped a huge pile of wood then he went around to the front garden and mowed the lawn. I stood at the wire door and watched him, his hat pushed back on his head, his shirt sleeves rolled up and a pair of striped braces to keep his pants up. When he finished, he put everything away, put on his jacket, which had been hanging in a tree, and left without a word. He disappeared. We grew up and my mother grew old.

We Find Bob

Thirty-five years later, my mother received a phone call from the Salvation Army men's hostel in Bendigo.

"Hello, is that Mrs Mack?"

"Yes," answered my mother.

"Do you know a Bob Mack?" said the voice,

"Yes, I did. Once," my mother replied tentatively.

"Well, he's been found living in the bush just out of Bendigo."

My brothers and I went to Bendigo to renew our relationship with Uncle Bob. Mum didn't come.

Bob had been living as a swagman in and around Bendigo all that time. As a local oddity he was well known, but no one knew his name. He'd lived in the bush in a makeshift tent with only bush animals for company. About once a month, he would push his bicycle into town to buy fresh food, tea and matches. He never received a pension until the Salvation Army made an application for him. So the money we always thought he had no longer existed. He had spent all the money my father had paid him for his half of the house they had inherited from their parents.

When we arrived at the hostel, Uncle Bob had gone for a walk. He took ages to return and was probably hoping to avoid us. I stood at a window waiting to catch a glimpse of him as he came in the gate.

I heard one of his rescuers, John, talking to my brothers.

"When we found him he was in a bad way, shivering, cold and wet. He was having trouble keeping a fire alight. His bedding was damp and he only had stale bread left to eat," said John.

"It's quite possible he wouldn't have lasted through the winter," said my brother Jack.

"No, I don't think he would have," said John. "We took him to the doctor who said his ticker's a bit dicky."

"It's a good thing he's here in this nice warm house," Jack replied.

"Yeah. He loves the tucker but hates the shower. We had to bribe him with a roast dinner to get his clothes off and get him to walk into the water. While he was washing himself, we pinched his smelly old clothes and burnt them," said John.

At this point, a small man wearing a long gabardine coat and a brown hand-knitted beanie walked through the back gate. He looked around like a nervous animal, spotted me at the window and ducked behind a wall. Without alerting anyone, I walked outside to find him.

"Bob, can I talk to you? I'm your niece, Margaret. I've come from Melbourne to see you."

"Oh," said Bob.

"I've brought you a fruit cake," I said, handing him a cake tin.

"Oh."

"Come inside and meet your family."

There were husbands, wives and children galore. Poor man. He was overwhelmed by the day. He sat and listened, rocking back and forth on his chair like a damaged child. His eyes kept darting to the window. Sometimes he stood up then sat down again. He was not at ease.

I went to visit him a few more times after that and I think he worked out who I was. His brother's only daughter, the little girl he gave the clock to thirty-five years ago, now grown up with her own children. He seemed to like me, probably because I always took home-made cakes to him.

I told him where I lived and, as he remembered the area from when he was a child, he seemed interested. "Would you like to come to my home for a visit?" I asked him one day. "We could walk around and look at all the places you recall."

"Oh yes," he said.

"Next time the men from the hostel are coming to Melbourne for the football, they can bring you to my place. I'll take care of you for the day. We can walk around the streets and you can see how much everything has changed."

He nodded but said nothing. He was not comfortable sitting and talking for very long. He suddenly stood up.

"Better be off then," he said, and off he went, head down, feet shuffling through the gate and away from us.

Once as we talked, he allowed me to look into his eyes. I saw an amazing depth of sadness. It shocked me deeply. I stopped talking and touched his hand. He pulled it away and went off for another walk.

He never came to my home. He died suddenly of a massive heart attack.

It was a very small, sad funeral. I cried, at last. For my father as well as poor old Uncle Bob, and the two neglected little boys of long ago. In his coffin, Bob wore the gabardine coat, the knitted beanie on his head. Soft white curls lay on his pale forehead. I chose the hymn Morning Has Broken, sung by Cat Stevens, to be played as we farewelled him in the chapel.

I thought of Bob in the bush at daybreak as the mist lifted and the birds sang their dawn chorus. I wondered if he had liked the bush or if he just liked to be alone. Apparently, his only companion had been a kangaroo that had visited him occasionally.

We had afternoon tea with the people in the hostel. They seemed like true Christians, not the pretend ones I was used to. They really cared for my uncle for the short time he was with them. I'm so glad they found him just in time. In the few months he was with them, I think he felt some of the kindness that had eluded him in his very sad lifetime.

His ashes are scattered in the bush.

I know this story sounds unbelievable but it is true and Bob did spend time living up on the roof. I have often wondered about the child who was born in Western Australia and is my first cousin.

Tommy

Tommy was the first person of the opposite sex who ever paid me any attention. I remember him peering up under my dress as I stood astride the monkey bars at school. I was wearing loose homemade knickers so he probably saw it all. Lucky Tommy.

He learnt singing and tap dancing on Saturday mornings at the local RSL hall. One Saturday I walked past the hall and I heard those children tapping and singing loudly to a piano, which banged out How Much is That Doggy in the Window? They sounded so happy.

"Mum, why can't I go? Why can't I learn to dance?" I asked her as we walked by.

"No daughter of mine is going to make an exhibition of herself like that," she declared in a voice loud enough for all to hear.

"It's not fair! It's not fair! It's not fair!" I chanted until the milk bar came into view.

"Can I have an ice-cream?" I asked.

"No."

"Oh, come on. Just a little one? Just a threepenny one?" I begged.

"No!"

"When I'm a mother, I'm going to buy my children an ice-cream every day," I yelled as loudly as I dared, keeping out of whacking distance.

One Saturday on his way home from his dancing lesson at the

RSL hall, Tommy called in to see me. He stood at the front gate and yelled, "Maaarrrr-gret!"

I was surprised he was calling for me and not one of my brothers.

"Why can't that child come to the front door and knock like any other normal human being?" Mum said.

I peered through the side window at the boy at the gate. Had he really come to see me? I had been in awe of him ever since I'd seen him singing and dancing at a recent school concert. I'd wanted so much to be that little baby-faced blonde girl who danced with him on the stage. I'd wanted to wear that short frilly dress that bounced up and down as she sang and tapped to Walking My Baby Back Home.

"He's wearing a suit with long trousers," I said to the girl sitting next to me.

"And she's wearing lipstick," the girl replied.

Continuing to sing, they came to the words "just when I try to straighten my tie" and Tommy did just that. He raised his hands and gently tugged at either side of his enormous red silk bow tie. He was so grown up for a ten-year-old boy and I thought he was wonderful. As the applause died down, he lifted his flushed face and flicked his soft curls out of his blue eyes. He looked out over the sea of faces, searching for a familiar face and, wonder of wonders, his eyes found mine. I stared at him my mouth agape, my eyes agog, unsophisticated me. In spite of that, I knew I would never be up there on that stage, dancing and singing with that beautiful fair-skinned boy with the dark wavy hair.

On the day Tommy came to visit me, my brother and his friend were playing in our large, overgrown back garden. They had made a boat out of an enormous old suitcase, the type that was used when travelling on a ship. They were attempting to rig up sails with an old sheet and a broom handle. The two boys smirked at Tommy so I stuck my tongue out at them as I ushered him down the garden path and up into the treehouse.

"Wait here," I said. "I'll get some biscuits."

Skipping inside I raided the biscuit tin and soon returned with the biscuits bulging in my pocket. I climbed the ladder into the treehouse but Tommy wasn't there.

"Where is he?" I asked the two older boys, now both sitting on top of the closed suitcase.

"He's gone," they said in unison.

"Why did he go?" I asked disappointed.

"Probably had to go and dance," my brother said, mincing across the path towards me.

"What do you mean?"

Their smirks turned into huge grins and then became loud riotous laughter. It was at this point I noticed that the suitcase was moving.

"Let me out," said a muffled voice.

"Have you put him in there?" I yelled, jumping down off the ladder.

"In where? In what?" the boys said, laughing even more.

"You've got Tommy in that suitcase, haven't you? Let him out. He won't be able to breathe."

The suitcase was rocking.

"He might die if he can't breathe. Open it," I begged.

The suitcase was really moving now. Picking up an old tennis racket the boys had been using as an oar, I began to swing at them.

"Get off! Get off! You're going to kill my friend," I yelled.

I jumped on top of the suitcase and, wielding the racket, I began to hit them. On the head. On the backside. Anywhere I could make contact, and it worked. Both of them fell back onto the grass laughing and falling over each other as they tried to get up. I gave them both a final swipe as they got to their feet. Screaming with laughter, they disappeared around the side of the house yelling at the top of their voices, "Ya bloody big sissy!"

I opened the catch and lifted the lid to let out the captive who, I assumed, would now follow me up into the tree house where we would eat our biscuits. How wrong I was. Unlike me, who had experienced similar behaviour from brothers and cousins on numerous occasions, this was a terrifying event for Tommy, an only child. Looking down at him as he struggled to keep from crying, he reminded me of a shivering rabbit I had once seen my uncle trap and kill. Poor Tommy. It had been an awful experience for him. He kept his eyes down and said nothing to me as he climbed out of the suitcase. Getting his footing at once, he followed the path of his captors towards the front garden, the gate and freedom.

"Goodbye Tommy," I said.

He didn't answer.

Hurrying to the front gate I leaned over just in time to see him fleeing down the hill towards home.

I saw him at school the next week. He was sitting up in the fork of a tree talking and laughing with a friend who sat higher up. He stopped laughing as I stood beneath the tree looking up at him, hoping for a smile. Glancing at me for just an instant, he quickly turned away and I knew that was the end of that.

The Red Traffic Light

The house was quiet. The doorbell rang. The baby woke. Should I answer the door or pick up the crying baby?

The baby pulled at my hair as I opened the door to a young policeman.

"Is your mother home?" he asked.

"No, she's out shopping."

"Will she be back soon?"

"I hope so. The baby is hungry," I said.

"I'll come back later." He moved his pushbike from our front gate to the gate next door.

From the window I watched him go into Mrs Roberts' house. Soon Mrs Roberts came rushing out. She looked up at our house then hurried over the road to where the Floyd family lived. I put the baby on the floor to play and began colouring in my book. The picture I was working on was a busy road full of cars, bicycles, trams and trucks. I was about to colour in the traffic lights when Mum's key turned in the lock.

"Mum, there was a policeman here to see you," I said.

"Really? What did he want?" she asked.

"I don't know but he went in to Mrs Roberts' place."

"Maybe she was able to help him. Can you help me to put the

shopping away please?"

"Okay," I said.

I began to pull out the parcels.

"What did you buy for dinner?" I asked.

Mum picked up the baby. "I have bought a treat—pies and pasties," she said.

"Yum, yum, pig's bum. I love pies and pasties."

"You will get nothing for dinner if you speak like that," Mum replied.

The doorbell rang. Mum opened the door. It was the policeman again. She took in his grim expression and straightened her shoulders.

My mother handed the baby to me.

"Go into the lounge room and keep the baby company," she said slowly.

I returned to my colouring book. With red pencil in hand, I started to colour the top light. I couldn't hear everything the policeman said but I did hear him say, "…when he was riding his bike to work."

"My dad rides a bike to work," I thought.

"He was hit by a truck," said the policeman.

A tear fell onto the page.

"He has been very seriously injured."

Silent tears rained down onto the busy road. The traffic light smudged. The whole page was ruined. I heard rapid footsteps on the front path. Our neighbour Mrs Floyd called out.

"Mrs Mack, I'll drive you to the hospital," she said.

Mum left without a word to me. She zoomed off in a green Humber car belonging to our neighbour. Someone took the baby, someone else took my two brothers after school and I was taken to stay with the Casset family down the road where my friend Trisha lived. They were kind people but very quiet and reserved. I didn't fully understand why I had to stay there and was too afraid of their answers to ask. They were always crossing themselves and saying prayers with beads. I was embarrassed at night time when they knelt in front of their shabby chairs and prayed to Mary Mother of God. I didn't know God had a mother. They were Catholics and I was a Baptist. I felt like an intruder but they were kind to me and I heard them pray for my family.

I didn't go to school for the duration of my stay with the Cassets. Long, quiet days stretched out endlessly. I had none of my own things with me, yet my home was only six houses up the hill. When Trisha came home from school, she was different.

"When can I go home?" I asked her.

"Don't worry, we will care for you. We will pray for you," she replied.

Thankfully, after several days my Aunty Mona came to get me.

"Hello Mrs Casset. I've come for Margaret. How is she?" said Aunty Mona.

"She's been so quiet and no trouble at all."

"I didn't think she would be. Thank you for your kindness," said Aunty Mona, and up the hill we went. I could have gone home on my own. I walked to school on my own. What on earth was this all about?

Home at last, but it was so different, so quiet. I sensed that I had to be very good. I stood nervously in my bedroom looking at nothing in particular. My mother came into the room at last. I had not seen her since the day she had left me with the baby to go shopping.

"What happened to the pies and pasties?" I asked her.

I knew at once this was not a good question. She just looked at me with sad eyes. My heart was beating so fast.

"How is Daddy?" I asked, my heart choking me.

"He's gone to be with his mother," said my mother.

She turned and left the room. I had never met Dad's mother. She died before I was born. Through a watery blur, I concentrated on a wooden knob on the cedar chest of drawers.

Outside my bedroom window there were two huge palm trees that housed hundreds of birds. Because it was late in the day, they were all bedding down for the night. The screeching, whistling and singing was amazing. They did it every morning and every night. I loved the sound. It is one of those things I always associate with my room at home and, sadly, that afternoon. I concentrated on the cacophony. It filled my head and my heart and helped me to ignore my pain.

Once I thought I was in a state of control like my mother, I ventured out of the room. I could hear my older brother Andrew talking quietly to our cat Puss.

"Nice Puss, soft Puss. Daddy has gone away and he's not coming back."

"Andrew? Andrew where are you?" I called.

"Here," came a little voice.

Andrew was curled up small on the large couch in the lounge room, the cat lying in his arms.

"Did you hear about Daddy?" I asked, sitting close to him.

"Yes," he replied, looking at me with moist, fearful eyes. He stroked the tortoiseshell cat. Lucky Puss. She was oblivious to it all. Like the adults around us, we said nothing more about it.

"Come on Andrew. Let's go to the cubby."

I knew we would feel better in there. Andrew picked up the cat and followed me into a large room at the front of the house. This room was used for storage of furniture that my parents did not wish to use in the house. There were tables, chairs, a cabinet, two Chinese screens and various other bits and pieces. From the doorway and reaching into every corner, we had blankets and old curtains draped all over the furniture, which made it a room full of dark tunnels and secret corners.

"Let's go inside," I said to Andrew.

Down on our hands and knees we crawled into the most distant corner where no adult could go. We lay down on cushions, the fat cat between us, a blanket pulled over our heads. We talked about what we would call the kittens when they were born. We were able to get lost in there.

Poor Andrew. Had he known what responsibility people wanted to put on his young shoulders, he would have looked even more fearful that night.

"Well young man, you'll have to grow up in a hurry," said a neighbour.

"You're the man of the house now," said another.

"You have to take responsibility for the younger children and help your mother now," said someone at the church.

Andrew was only nine years old. What on earth were they all thinking?

Puss had her four kittens in the laundry: two tortoiseshell, two black and white. What a godsend. We loved those kittens so much. We hurried home from school each day longing to see them. The tiny little things with their eyes still closed mewed at their mother who fed and licked them constantly. When they struggled to their feet, they wobbled and fell over and mewed some more. We picked them up and stroked them. We kissed them on their little heads and gave them new names every day. We adored them. One day when we came home from school Puss was waiting for us at the front gate. She meowed at us.

"Why aren't you with your babies?" I asked her.

She meowed some more.

"Come on Puss. I suppose you got locked out."

Into the laundry we went. No kittens, no box. Nothing.

"Mum? Where are the kittens?" I yelled.

"What have you done with them?" Andrew wailed.

"Mr Jones took them away for us," she replied.

"Not for us. We want them. Tell him we want them back," I cried, losing control. Andrew was in a similar state. We clung to each other crying for our kittens and our daddy.

"Don't be silly. I told you last week when they were born that we couldn't keep them," said Mum.

"Yes, but we thought you had changed your mind."

"Well I haven't, and if Andrew had done what I asked, this would not have happened."

What she had asked him to do was unthinkable. She had wanted him to drown the kittens.

"Andrew, now that your father is no longer with us, you will have to do some of his jobs," she had said to him.

"What do you want, Mum?" said poor little Andrew.

"I want you to drown the kittens."

"No," said Andrew, not really believing she meant it.

"Just take them to the toilet, put them in one at a time and pull the chain."

"No, I can't do that! I don't want to," said Andrew.

"Well, who do you think is going to do it if you don't?"

"I don't know," said Andrew, beginning to cry.

"If you are going to grow up to be a man you will have to do some things that you don't like doing."

Poor Andrew. He was so confused and unhappy.

"Maybe I do have to do this," he thought.

After a lot of persuasion by my mother, he did as he was told. I will never forget him running back towards the house, tears streaming down his distraught little face. He carried the kittens in his arms. One appeared to be half drowned and it struggled and mewed in his hands. We dried it off and returned all the kittens to their mother.

"It kept swimming and it wouldn't go down. It was awful," he wailed.

I locked the laundry door from the inside. We stayed with Puss until she had licked the kitten all over, fed it and it was sleeping peacefully. Mum said nothing about the kittens so we thought she had decided to let them live. We had a week to bond with them and then they disappeared.

Fun In The Garden

Eventually the gloom began to lift and our lives regained some sort of normality. My brothers and I were a mischievous little group. Apart from Andrew, there was George, who is two years younger than me, and baby Jack, who was usually asleep. We often played on the front veranda, which was very long, stretching from one side of the house to the other. One end was my house and the other end was my brothers' house. I pretended to have a daughter called Maryanne and she was always forgetting to put on her underpants before going to school. Not really very funny, but we always found it hilarious and laughed and laughed. Mum said we were silly but she laughed also. There were two old wicker lounges on the veranda, which had been brought from Hong Kong when my grandparents moved to Australia. One was a rocker, which we pulled onto the grass and we rocked on it so much and so hard that it fell apart and Mum burnt it. As for the other one, we somehow wore a hole in the seat and that made it useless and it too had to be burnt. We were allowed to play pretty much unrestricted, which was a good thing. I think.

One evening in the summer, we were squirting each other with the hose in the front garden. People walked past our home on their way from the train station. The temptation to squirt these hot exhausted people as they passed by was too strong to resist. So, we did it. We squirted them. The fence was lined by a hedge, so any water that wet these tired people could easily have been accidental. We would follow the wetting with, "Oh sorry," or "I didn't see you," or "I beg your pardon." Giggle, giggle.

It became very contrived. One of us hung over the gate to see who was coming, one manned the tap ready to turn it on full pelt and the other held the hose.

"Here comes Mr Appleby," said Andrew. "Let's squirt him."

Mr Appleby was a strange little man who lived with his maiden sister down the hill on the corner. He had a large bald head and sometimes he giggled nervously like a child. When he wasn't talking, he would roll his huge tongue around inside his cheeks. Sometimes it would pop out of his mouth. It was pretty gross. We often called into his house on the way home from Sunday school and church on the pretext of looking for our mother.

"Is Mum here, Mr Appleby?"

"No. Perhaps she is already at home. Would you like a biscuit?"

"Oh, yes. Thank you."

This is really why we went there. He had jam biscuits with the face of the sun on them.

"Take two," he'd say.

"Oh, thank you very much. Mum is probably home by now. Goodbye," and we would tear up the hill, chomping on the biscuits.

We became very bold with the hose that hot evening. Mr Appleby was about our tenth victim. We were pretty good at it by then. We waited patiently for his footsteps on the footpath. He was about halfway down the length of the fence, almost to the gate when Andrew signalled to George at the tap. George turned on the water. The water came out with such force it sent Mr Appleby's hat flying off his head and into the gutter. He muttered something about bloody kids as he walked towards the hat. I had become so confident in this squirting game I decided to finish it off with a bang. Getting ready to run I aimed the hose at his large backside as he was bending over to retrieve his hat and yelled at the top of my voice: "Cop that Mr Applebum." We tore around the back and up into the tree house, laughing till our bellies hurt.

Mum called from inside, "Would one of you children water the garden please?"

"We already did it," I called out.

Mum was very angry when she found out about us squirting Mr Appleby. When we were older, we discovered that Mr Appleby was a paedophile so I'm glad we did squirt him.

There were three paedophiles at our church, but people were too ignorant or innocent to acknowledge it. As a teenager, my brother Jack decided to do something about it. He called in to see the minister and told him what he knew. The minister was horrified and assured Jack he would address the situation. The next Sunday we went to church and were amused but not really surprised at the minister's way of dealing with the problem. He preached a sermon on the sins of Sodom and Gomorrah. That was all. We laughed all the way home and never went to church again. It's no wonder I am a cynic.

As I have grown older, I've tried to understand my mother and why she behaved the way she did with us, and the cats. My mother was a good woman, brought up by strict religious parents who had no time for her feelings. Showing your feelings was considered self-indulgent and soft, yet she was always expected to be considerate of other people. Even when she was hurt, she was not allowed to cry. She had to take responsibility for her younger siblings and was punished if they did not do their piano or violin practice. She spent her childhood in the country where animals were a commodity and not cared for as they are today.

All of this, coupled with her untimely widowhood, made my mother act in the most practical way without considering feelings or consequences. I look back now and can see that she loved us but was so traumatised by my father's death that she sometimes barely coped. My parents had only been married for ten years when he died and my brothers and I were one, five, seven and nine years old. It was difficult and it was sad and sometimes extremely bleak, but we got through it. Unfortunately, I cannot say that we escaped unaffected by our sad childhood.

In spite of my grandparents being excessively strict parents, they mellowed as they aged and never seemed stern to me. I think Grandpa was really fond of me and because I was unhappy and too thin, he said he would like me to stay with them for the school holidays so he could fatten me up. Every morning he made porridge for me topped with honey and cream from the top of the milk. At dinnertime he always made chips for me and cooked pork sausages because I liked them. They lived in Elwood and sometimes we walked to Elsternwick so he could buy the sausages for me. He always wore a suit, a bowler hat and carried an umbrella. He didn't carry a bag for the sausages. He put them into his briefcase. He looked like an English gentleman. In the afternoon, he would sit at the piano and play Beethoven very loudly and when he had finished, he would play and sing the national anthem. We did have a queen but he always seemed to forget and sang, "God Save the King". He also told stories and accompanied the tale with appropriate music. He was quite a character. And yes, I did put on weight.

Mum told me that during the Depression in the nineteen-thirties, my grandfather always had either a pot of soup or a hearty stew on the stove ready to eat. It was common for unemployed young men roaming the countryside to knock on the door offering to work for a bite to eat or some shelter. Mum said my grandfather fed many of these unfortunate people. During a cold winter one man really tugged at my grandfather's heart strings, so much so that he gave him his new overcoat, which my grandmother had just made for him. Grandmother was not happy, she had scrimped and saved to buy the material and as they were not wealthy there would not be another new coat for a long time.

When I was about thirteen, one of my school friends had a cat with kittens. I went after school to see them and she offered one to me. Without asking my mother I chose a tortoiseshell female. When it was time to take her home, I put her in my school bag and took her home with me on the tram. I was very surprised at Mum's reaction.

"What a nice little kitten," she said.

I called her Brigitte after the famous Brigitte Bardot. We had her neutered and she lived happily for about fifteen years. Was my mother sorry for what had happened earlier? Had she forgotten or had she just changed? Whatever the answer, she loved Brigitte and enjoyed her company by the fire and in the garden. I was a married woman when Brigitte died and Mum rang to tell me. I could swear she had been crying. I went to see my sweet-natured cat before my brother buried her. I put some daisies into the box she was to be buried in and I felt very sad. There is no doubt that animals are an enormous and important part of our lives and just like people we don't forget them.

Sunday School

I started Sunday School at about four years of age and I clearly remember my first day. It was a warm, sunny day sometime in January. I was wearing a pretty pink dress Mum had made for the occasion. Mum managed to tie a ribbon in my hair as I jumped up and down impatiently. Then, holding my older brother's hand, we skipped and ran down the hill towards the local church. My brother took me into a building adjoining the church and handed me to a pleasant-looking young woman who was the teacher of the Sunday School kindergarten. As she took my hand and led me across to a sunny little side room, I felt that while I had her attention I had better quickly impress her with my worthiness to be at Sunday School.

"It's good that I'm coming to Sunday School because my grandfather was a minister and he was a missionary in Africa, and he used to ride a pony, and he saw a Zulu with a big spear and lions," I gushed.

Looking up at her I was pleased to see I had made her smile.

There were about twenty other children in the room sitting on small chairs. The girls were mostly wearing pretty summery dresses like mine, short white socks and black patent leather shoes. My shoes had tiny blue flowers joined with fine green stitching across the toes. They were very special.

The teacher told us a story about Jesus and we sang a little song, then the teacher said a prayer to Jesus. One little boy didn't close his eyes so I told the teacher. That made her smile again.

My brothers and I went to Sunday School every Sunday morning whether we liked it or not. By the time I was about ten, I did not like it so it was probably my idea to wag Sunday School the first time. As we set off in our Sunday best, Mum would give us each sixpence to put in the plate for Jesus. Being a sceptic from a very young age, I had my doubts that Jesus was spending any time at our church or Sunday School. I certainly had not seen anyone fitting his description: shoulder-length hair, long flowing robes and sandals. I reckon the congregation would have thrown anyone who looked like that right out the door. It was the fifties after all, and they were a very conservative lot.

On this particular day, we went down the hill and around the corner as usual but instead of continuing along to the church, we took a sharp turn to the right and ran down the hill towards the milk bar. In those days, you could buy quite a lot with sixpence. Various lollies were ten a penny, eight a penny, four a penny or two a penny, enough to satisfy any child or make any child sick. We bought a bag of mixed lollies each and walked down a lane to eat them in secret. We were forbidden to go into lanes on our own but we did not want to be seen by any of the goody-goodies who might be going to Sunday School or, even worse, their parents going to church. This particular lane was especially off limits because there was an SP bookmaker who operated there and my mother did not like the look of the men who frequented the area. We decided to look for the SP bookie as we strolled down the lane eating our lollies and peeping through gaps in the fences or gates that had been left open.

Being a Sunday, there were no races and hence no betting, but we did not know that. We came to a partly open gate and cautiously peered around the palings only to come face-to-face with Mrs Day, who was hanging washing on the line. Mrs Day was the mother of Kay, the biggest goody-goody and smarty-pants in Sunday School. Kay could recite the Ten Commandments in order, she knew the Lord's Prayer, the benediction and God knows what else. She was overweight, wore glasses and loved to tell tales. What bad luck that we should find Mrs Day at her back gate.

"Why aren't you two at Sunday School?" Mrs Day boomed at us.

"We are not going today," I replied. "Mum knows."

"Does your mum know that you've spent your offering to Jesus on lollies?"

I just stared at her. How do grownups always know these things I thought?

I whispered to my brother, "Run."

We ran up the hill to the church, not sure what to do. We had not thought past buying the lollies. Should we go in and say we had forgotten our offering, or perhaps we could say we lost it? Better still, we could wait outside the church door till Mum came, go in with her, tell her we had lost our money and we preferred to sit with her instead of the Sunday School children.

We could see Mum coming down the hill and turning the corner towards the church. She was wearing her grey coat and pink hat and gloves. We were about to run up to her when who should turn the corner from down the hill? Mrs Day. They met halfway and walked the remaining distance together. Mum did not look happy as she approached us. She made us stay with her for the entire service, which we hated. We had to sing four hymns and endure the children's sermon and the grownups' sermon and God knows how many prayers. Then we had to apologise to the minister for spending the money for Jesus on lollies. After that we had to sit with Mum in church every week.

There were quite a few older women usually sitting behind us who wore funny hats and seemed so old. When they sang the hymns in their high wobbly voices, I could not help turning around to see who was making the funny warbling sound. It made me giggle. Mum said it was rude to stare and even ruder to laugh at their excellent attempts at singing. In an effort to stop giggling and to ease the boredom of church, I would sing the hymns backwards or whistle the tune quietly. Mum quickly put an end to that. I tried to sneak a book in to read during the long tedious hour. That was also forbidden. I just had to endure it.

On one occasion, the service was so tedious I went into a trance. I remember staring so hard at the choir members that a halo began to appear around each of their heads. I thought they could have been angels and was expecting wings to appear at any minute. The minister started yelling loudly about sinners going to hell and I came out of my trance. The spell was broken and the angels never appeared. I'm not sure how I saw those halos. Perhaps I had a temperature and was hallucinating.

I continued to go to Sunday School every week with very little enthusiasm. At the end of the lesson, the teacher would give us a verse from the Bible to learn for the following week. We were expected to recite the verse at the beginning of the lesson the next week. I always forgot about learning the verse the minute I left and only remembered the following week when I saw the other students reciting theirs and taking their reward for being such good little children. When faced with this situation, my plan was to always get to the end of the line so that I was the last to be heard. That way, I was usually able to recite the verse without the teacher knowing I had just learnt it from everyone else as they recited theirs before me. The reward was a stamp (or sticker we call them now) with a picture of Jesus doing something good or miraculous from one of the stories in the New Testament. We put the stamps into a book the church provided. Mine never filled up.

Each year the Sunday School held exams for the older children. My brother had taken part and now that I was old enough, it was expected by the teachers (and my mother), that I would also sit the exams.

"Margaret, you can sit the exams this year," said Miss Smith.

My older brother always did well so they all thought I would too.

"No. I don't want to," I replied.

"Yes, you will. I have already spoken to your mother and she agrees with me," said Miss Smith.

I mumbled that no one listened to me and proceeded to head home.

"Mum, Miss Smith says I have to do exams at Sunday School and I don't want to."

"Well, you will do the exams and that's all there is to it," she replied sternly.

Under my breath, I muttered, "They can't make me. They can't make me."

They did make me though, and it was a waste of time and paper because I did not study and I guessed the answers, which were wrong anyway. Largely, the questions consisted of a narrative with blanks to fill in with the appropriate people or places. Mary and Martha were the most common female names I used and Jesus, Moses, Noah and John were the only names I could think of at the time. Perhaps Samson and Delilah had a mention also. I felt dreadful because I knew my efforts were in vain. I had said I didn't want to sit the silly exams; why they couldn't have listened to me I don't know.

As time went by, I did not think much about the exams but as I had filled in all the spaces, I began to think I had probably got a few correct. In fact, after a while I began to think I had probably done quite well.

I was wrong, and the way I found out was at the end-of-year Sunday School presentation night. The superintendent of the Sunday School, Mr Starchy, made a speech which included the following:

"It is with great regret and deep shame that I have to announce that for the first time in the long history of the Sunday School, we have been let down by one of our students. Not only did this person not pass the exams, but managed to disgrace us by failing to answer any questions correctly. The failure has ended a long history of success and excellence from our Sunday School pupils. We will pray to God to help this student get a better result next year."

"Well," I thought, "he can't mean me because I filled in all the spaces. I must have got some right."

But he did mean me, because he presented a book to everyone at Sunday School except me. I had to face it. I did not even get an award for trying. Mind you, when I saw the book my brother got, I didn't care much. We already had enough books about the Bible and Jesus. Obviously, I had not been reading them.

Mum did not say a word to me about the disgrace and no one ever asked me to do Sunday School exams again. Thank the Lord Jesus.

Another annual event was the Sunday School picnic. On a Saturday morning in springtime, all the children of the Sunday School and some parents were driven far away to the other side of Melbourne for a day in the country. They transported us in huge removalist trucks with long seats fitted for the journey. We went to places like Warrandyte or Wattle Park which, in the fifties, were still in the country. I remember the bushland, a creek, the magpies, cockatoos and flies. One year, two boys were lost for several hours and everyone was worried they may have fallen down a cliff or been bitten by a snake. Several men went off searching for them and those of us who remained behind prayed for their safe return. They were found safe and sound miles away up the dry creek bed. They had wanted to see where it went. As we ate our sandwiches and drank our cordial, we were told that God had delivered them back to the fold. I knew it wasn't God but two men who had set out to find them who returned the two boys to us. They couldn't fool me.

The Sunday School had a concert or talent quest each year and as I seemed able to sing, I was always roped in to sing the Brahms Lullaby or Whistle a Happy Tune from The King and I. As I got older, I didn't want to sing these daggy songs, so when my teacher asked me to sing, I told her my voice had broken and I was unable to sing any more. She gave me a strange look as if she knew I was telling a fib. Once again, she appealed to my mother and, once again, my mother agreed that I would take part.

I thought, "They never listen to me. I'll show them this time."

The night of the concert came and I was sitting in the audience waiting for my turn to sing. Someone announced my name and I walked up the stairs to the stage. There were a lot of people watching including my mother, my Sunday School teacher, the minister and the Sunday School superintendent. Everyone actually. I stood centre stage, opened my mouth and began to sing without the music. They expected Brahms' Lullaby, instead they got a popular song by Buddy Holly.

"There you go and baby, here am I.
Well, you left me here so I can sit and cry.
Well, oops-a-daisy how you drove me crazy.
Well, I guess it doesn't matter any more..."

When I finished singing, there was dead silence. It was just a bit too much for all those puritans. Remember, rock 'n roll was considered music of the devil when it first began. Everyone was staring at me and then one teenage boy, obviously a kindred spirit, cheered and clapped, which encouraged a few other meagre claps. Once again, Mum said nothing. Needless to say, I was not asked to sing at the Sunday School concert ever again.

Within the congregation there were three paedophiles. I know this for a fact because one of them tried to get into bed with my brother when they were at a boys' camp. Another of the paedophiles took my brother's friend to the riverside park at night-time instead of taking him home. The friend used to make jokes I didn't understand at the time about something splashing on the dashboard. He said they were not there to study the nocturnal animals. The third paedophile liked to drive a particular young girl home after night-time Bible study. Not me, thank goodness. We lived just around the corner and I could walk home. Actually, I think it's obvious I didn't go to Bible study.

As far as I can remember, there were three different ministers at the church while my brothers and I were involved there. The first one, tall dark and handsome, was Mr Warden, who increased the size of the female congregation overnight. There was pretty young Mrs Warden whom the large, adoring female congregation could only admire and imagine they were in her shoes. Mr Warden was a liberal-minded man who allowed a bit of fun in the church. We sang and clapped hands to religious songs; we had calisthenics classes and concerts in the hall, boys' clubs, girls' clubs and games nights. It was quite an enjoyable time really, but it did not last. After only a few years, Mr Warden was moved to another church in Kew and we got a new minister called Mr Larkins, and he was a large shock.

Mr Larkins was a big surprise to everyone. He was the absolute opposite to his handsome, quietly-spoken predecessor. We now had a big man with a big voice who conducted long sermons full of fire and brimstone which were meant to frighten us into being better Christians. It did frighten me. I was scared of the dark and scared to go to sleep at night in case I should die in my sleep. There was no more singing and clapping hands, there were no more clubs for boys or girls. The calisthenics ended and the calisthenics teacher moved to Kew where the Wardens now lived. It became a very sombre place. The female congregation shrank. In fact, the whole congregation shrank. But not us, we still went.

Mr Larkins was very like my grandfather in his attitude towards religion and life in general. What I mean is, he was very strict and had unrealistic expectations of people. Because my mother was used to this kind of man, she didn't seem to notice or care. Plus, the church was just around the corner from us. Very handy, even though Mum was a Methodist; she had decided this church was very similar.

One of the things the church and Sunday School did was to support a group of missionaries in central Australia. We were encouraged to give unwanted clothes, toiletries and toys and to raise money for the children in this institution. It was called Yuendumu and I always remember being told about the poor little orphaned black children who lived there. Now, as an adult and since the shame of the stolen generations have become well known, I feel some guilt and I am shocked to realise that we were usually not supporting orphans but children wrenched from their families. Such a tragedy.

I only stayed on at Sunday School for a year or two more until one Sunday morning when I was fourteen. I lay in bed waiting for my mother to call me to get up.

"Come on Margaret. Get up now or you will be late," called Mum.

I just lay there thinking, "What if? What if?"

"Come on," she yelled again.

"No," I said.

"No, what?" she replied.

"No. I am not going."

"Why not?"

"Because I don't want to go any more and I am not going," I said.

"Well, that was easy," I thought. "Why didn't I do that ages ago?"

There were people at the church who loved to keep a look out for us and report any perceived wrongdoing to our mother. I call them stickybeaks and troublemakers and I know now there were worse things going on at the church than boys and girls talking and laughing together on street corners. When I was about ten years old, Mrs Day overheard me telling some children that a boy's dicky was like a sausage and, as I had three brothers, I knew what I was talking about. She threatened to tell my mother, saying that I had been "talking dirty" with boys.

I told Mum as I thought it would be wise to get in early and give my side of the story. When Mrs Day told Mum, she was still cross with me but there was no punishment and I heard Mum and her friend Mrs Jones laughing as she related the story to her.

Walking home from school one day with a friend, we met up with a boy my friend liked. She tried to impress him with her knowledge of relationships between men and women. I think the word sex must have been uttered because a voice from behind us said, "You had better get home girly and read your Bible."

I looked over my shoulder and there was Mrs Rosa. Poor, sad, nasty Mrs Rosa.

"I'll be telling your mother about this. I heard what you were talking about." She didn't seem to care that it was not me doing the talking. I told Mum, who told me to get out of her sight and to behave myself.

Then there was Mr Booker who saw me waiting for my younger brother after we had been to the afternoon picture theatre. Two boys stopped to talk to me and I was laughing, heaven forbid, as Mr Booker drove past.

"You are a disgrace to your poor mother. You had better get home, young lady," he yelled at me.

There is a moral to this story. These people all had children of their own and two of their children did things later in life that were criminal and/or wrong. One had an affair with a teenage student he was teaching and the other raped a young girl.

The third minister, Mr Hunter, came to the church long after I had left. He was another sheltered man who did not cope well with the realities of life. It was he who my youngest brother went to regarding the paedophiles at the church. Mr Hunter said he would deal with it. The following Sunday he preached a sermon on the Bible story about Sodom and Gomorrah.

My middle brother, George, married his first wife when she was six months pregnant. Mr Hunter performed the ceremony in the manse, not the church, because an unmarried pregnant woman would defile the sanctity of the church. (I happen to know that the church had already been defiled when some boys were assaulted in there by one of the paedophiles.) In those days, boys were told not to touch themselves so they must have got a shock when they were allowed to touch a trusted church elder as he touched them.

The man who raped the young girl got off very lightly because of Mr Hunter's intervention to guarantee treatment and supervision, etc. The rapist was a sad person who was abused both emotionally and physically as a boy. He had no friends and he did not look too good either. What about the poor fatherless girl who had a fatherless baby at sixteen? I don't know what happened to her.

Some of the women at the church knew that to protect their children they had to keep them away from certain people, but I don't think they really knew what these men were capable of. When I was in my thirties, I told my mother the grim truth about the sexual abuse of boys by these men and she was shocked. She had no idea, and I suspect this was the norm because people did not talk openly about anything so shocking and unpleasant in those days.

For all his faults, I have one good thing to say about Mr Hunter. George's baby was born prematurely and died at a few weeks of age. Mr Hunter performed the service and although I had long lost my belief in God, the words he used to console us were very comforting. I walked away almost believing that the poor little darling was in heaven.

Of my family, only one of my brothers continued to attend church and Mum kept going as long as she was able to walk up the hill to get home. My brother, who called himself a Christian, would not drive her there even though he was living in her house. So, she stayed at home and read her Bible and received weekly visits from the minister. Mum always read her Bible each night before going to sleep. And she died believing she would go to heaven. As I said at her funeral, if there is a heaven she will probably be there.

When I was about to begin training as a nurse, I needed a character reference from a minister of religion. I only had access to one minister of religion so I made an appointment to see Mr Larkins. We sat in the lounge room of the manse and chatted about what I was going to do with my life and about young people in general. He obviously saw me as a source of information for some questions which were bothering him.

"Is it true," he asked, "that young people are having sexual relations outside marriage?"

"Oh yes," I said.

"That's terrible," he replied.

"Yes," I answered.

"Do you think they know that in the eyes of God they are fornicators?"

"I don't know."

"Do you know anyone who is indulging in this sinful behaviour?" he asked.

"Yes, I do," I replied, and turned a bright red colour.

"Oh, I am sorry to embarrass you," he stuttered. "I will write you a reference for the hospital and send it to you."

"Thank you," I replied, standing and walking quickly towards the door.

I escaped and ran home not sure whether I should laugh or not.

Of course, I knew people who were having premarital sex. It was the sixties and we had the Pill and I was taking it and I was doing it. So that meant even he knew someone who was sinning in this way. He just didn't know it.

I trained as a nurse and this finally ended any religious beliefs still lingering in my head. Seeing good, religious people dying awful, painful deaths, innocent babies born with horrific deformities or cancer, the death of my father and my mother's sad life have left me not believing in any god. Although I dislike organised religion, I still like the ethics of Christianity.

Do unto others as you would have them do unto you.

The Street Where We Lived

There were about twenty houses on each side of our short street. On our side, the houses were all Victorian and on the other side they were Edwardian and Californian bungalows. The properties were all quarter-acre blocks with attractive gardens at the front and vegetable gardens, fruit trees and chickens in the back yards. At the time I was a very young child there were very few cars and we could play on the road for hours without having to move off. We played tennis, cricket and football, and in 1956 we played the Olympic Games. Some children had billy carts, which they rode down the hill and whizzed around the corner at high speed. All the families knew each other and the children all played together.

Our house and the two to the north of us were the oldest in the street and had been built around 1880 to house local government employees and their families. They were solid brick with bluestone foundations and contained large rooms with high ceilings and grand fireplaces. At the side of the fireplaces there were bells, which in the past could be pressed to summon the maid. We did not have a maid of course, and we drove my mother mad ringing the bells so much that she demanded my father disconnect them—to our great annoyance. In the back yard, we had a large carriage shed and stables which became my father's work and storage shed.

Next door to us lived the nicest family. They were extremely kind to my mother and us after my father died. When Mum was sick, Mrs Roberts cooked dinner for us and she allowed Mum to use their telephone whenever she needed to. Mrs Roberts was a seamstress, and I remember one year she made me a warm pleated skirt. Her sister, who lived with her, knitted me a pretty pink jumper, both of which I loved. I wore the skirt and jumper as long as possible. In the end I just had to admit that they were both too small for me.

It was post-WWII, and there were six spinsters who had lost loved ones in the war, each living alone in their own houses. I suppose this would have been reflected throughout the world at the time. These women all worked fulltime and seemed to keep to themselves. One of them, Miss Allen, surprised us all by suddenly announcing that she was to be married. The news of the approaching wedding gave everyone something to talk about and it seemed to make people happy because it was rumoured that Miss Allen had been engaged to marry a man who had died in a Japanese prisoner of war camp.

She always wore a blue hat and coat, and little bits of blonde hair could be seen escaping from her hat. That's how I remember her, until the day she emerged from her front door totally transformed as a beautiful bride. To me as a little girl she looked like a princess, her pretty blonde hair around her face and falling down to her shoulders. Her white dress was decorated with lace and heavily beaded, and she wore a veil down her back which touched the ground and had to be carried by her sister, who was dressed in a pale blue dress and hat. The bouquet Miss Allen carried was a huge bunch of white flowers with long trails of ivy. I couldn't believe she was the same woman. Everyone who lived in the street was at their fence oohing and aahing at her, and many of the neighbours gave her good luck charms and little blue things on loan. As the saying goes:

Something old, Something new,
Something borrowed, Something blue.

No one had seen the groom and we were all hanging out to see what he looked like. He came to live in his wife's house after they were married and looked like every other man at the time. He drove a Holden car and he wore a hat and a double-breasted suit to work, and that's about all I could say about him. Miss Allen was now Mrs Steele and I must say she looked much happier for a while, until Mr Steele died very suddenly from a heart attack and poor Mrs Steele was alone again. That gave everyone something to talk about for a while until we realised that Mrs Steele was going to be a mother and that was really good news and gave us even more to speculate about. All the women in the street rallied around and gave her an old pram, a cot, and numerous baby clothes and toys. Whether she wanted them or not, all people's unwanted baby goods were offloaded to poor Mrs Steele.

It was at this point that I began to take an interest in where babies came from and I bombarded my mother with questions about how the baby got in there and how on earth it would get out.

"Look," said Mum, "I haven't got time to tell you now but on Saturday morning, if you come and help me in the laundry, we will have a talk about it then."

Mum knew I hated helping her with the laundry so she was probably hoping I would be somewhere else on Saturday morning, but she was wrong. This was something I had to get to the bottom of.

"Well, Mum, how are babies made?" I asked, as I turned the wringer to squeeze excess water from the sheets.

"It's something very special," she said, "between a husband and wife."

"So do you have to be married to have babies?"

"Yes."

I know Mum was prepared to leave it there but I wasn't satisfied with her answer.

"Yes, but how does it happen?"

"The husband plants a seed," said Mum.

"A seed? What sort of seed, and where does he plant it?"

"Inside his wife," she answered.

I had done quite a bit of gardening with my parents so I had visions of tomato seeds or something similar being planted somewhere and was just about to push for a more accurate explanation when my younger brother George rode his tricycle down the back steps and knocked out his front teeth. I'm not saying Mum was happy about this mishap, but I think she was glad to get away from my in-depth questions. My little brother screamed for hours until Mum gave him half an Aspro in honey. He slept for ages and she thought the Aspro had killed him. She hadn't killed him. He woke up a few hours later and screamed some more.

That wasn't the first time I had heard him scream like that. When he was born he was quite a sick baby, something to do with his lungs. Therefore, when he was a neonate, he was not circumcised as all baby boys were in those days. When he was about eighteen months old, Mum took him to the local clinic to have the procedure done. It was done without any anaesthetic. He was just held down and the foreskin was snipped off. I know this because I was there. The poor little thing screamed and screamed in pain and after the procedure Mum sat in a chair trying to calm him. I was about four years old and wanted to get out of there so I was nagging and trying to get Mum's attention. I held on to the back of the chair she was sitting on and began to swing which quickly caused the chair to overbalance and fall back onto the floor. Mum, the screaming baby and I were sprawled on the floor when the nurse came in to check on the wound. Mum and I were crying by now so it must have been quite a sight. In the following weeks, my brother walked around with no pants on to help his poor little mutilated penis heal. Mum tried to keep him in the back garden but he liked to go to the front gate where he was the object of interest for a short time.

We had a family of Italian migrants who lived two doors up from us who were very friendly and once invited me to a pre-wedding party. I sat in a room full of women and was offered a green drink in a little glass. I looked at the bright green drink which I imagined to be delicious and instead of sipping it, I downed it in one gulp. It didn't taste the way I had expected and I coughed and spluttered, causing quite a stir of amusement and concern in the room. When I went home, I boasted to my brothers that I'd had a glass of delicious green wine and that I was probably drunk, but not sure. I was never quite sure why I was invited to the pre-wedding drinks with the Italian women but my aunt said they were probably considering me for one of their boys.

This same family had six children and when the little boys were toddlers they wore trousers that had the seams split from the front right through to the back, exposing their penises and little bottoms. As they were toilet training, I think it's a very good idea now, but it was unheard of in straitlaced Melbourne in the fifties. I remember going to the fence to talk to them so I could see their uncircumcised penises hanging out of their split seams. They were the sweetest little children, always smiling and laughing. I laughed too because it was funny.

Across the road lived a family who owned a delicatessen in Puckle Street and on Saturday after the shop shut the owner would bring a parcel of sausages or a chicken for my mother to cook. This was after my father had died and it was a good, kind thing he did for us. Once when Mum cooked the chicken, she forgot it and burnt it to a piece of charcoal. Me and my big mouth told the man's daughter that Mum had burnt the chicken but that it didn't matter because we had so much food anyway as the butcher had given us a leg of lamb. We never received another thing from the delicatessen family, not a sausage.

A very nice family moved in next door to the delicatessen people and they became great friends. They were such good friends that they put a gate in their adjoining side fence to allow easy access for their girls to play together and whatever other socialising they had in mind. They were all members of a happy-clappy church that had started up nearby and was run by a minister who wore long white robes and sometimes spoke in tongues. I went to the services sometimes because I dearly wanted to hear these strange utterances, but I never did hear anything unusual. In the end I lost interest because I met my first boyfriend. After a few months, he told me we could not be girlfriend and boyfriend because I was too young for him, which was true. One of the girls from the happy-clappy church told miserable me not to worry because Jesus would be my boyfriend.

I looked at her and thought, "Yeah, right."

She had obviously never had a real live boyfriend.

Anyway, something unpleasant happened between the two families across the road and the gate between the two households was suddenly bolted on both sides and no one from either family ever talked to each other again.

I heard Mrs Jones say to Mum, "I knew no good would come of that."

Next door to us lived Mr and Mrs Burr who were both pharmacists. They had no children but did have a Dalmation dog called Giggles who didn't giggle but jumped around and up and down the fence when it heard us playing outside. During autumn when Mr Burr raked up the fallen leaves to burn, Mum would get really annoyed because there was a large amount of dog poo in with the leaves and it stank. Mum would shut the doors and windows and rant because she couldn't put out the washing as it would smell awful when it dried in the smelly air.

Mr Burr died and Mrs Burr became ill. I think she had bone cancer or something very serious and painful, which caused her to become housebound and virtually bedridden. Mum did some shopping for her, and a neighbour across the road provided her with evening meals for some time. Her brother visited her occasionally. Mrs Burr read voraciously and Mum would go to the library every week to keep her supplied with books—she was reading about one a day. Mum lent her all of our books as well. Sometimes she would get out of bed and play the piano but as her illness progressed, she was unable to walk and used a wheelchair to go to the toilet or make herself something to eat. She always had a flask of boiling water beside the bed to make herself a cup of tea. In order for us to get into her house, she would leave the front door ajar for a few hours a day, otherwise we would speak to her through her bedroom window. It was her wish to remain in her home and she continued like this for many months.

Mum would tell me to go and see how Mrs Burr was and take her this jam or that cake.

So I had quite a few conversations with Mrs Burr either at her bedside or through the window. One day, Mum was unable to rouse her and after trying several times during the day, she rang the police who broke in and found her dead. She had been a smoker and when she died, she must have had a cigarette alight because it had burnt part of her bedding, but fortunately it did not burn her or cause any other damage. Mrs Burr had promised Mum a Wedgewood urn which sat on the her hall table, but Mrs Burr's sister-in-law refused to give it to her. She gave her a very unattractive pot and saucer instead. Mum did not get too upset about that because she was not materialistic, but she did say that had she should have taken it when Mrs Burr had first offered it.

Down the hill was the Jones family who were very good friends to my mother. They had a beautiful daughter called Hannah who suffered from muscular dystrophy and had great difficulty walking. She worked in the railway building near Spencer Street Station and each day her father and another neighbour walked her to the train station and into her office, where she worked for as long as she was able. Even though she was severely disabled, she made an effort to enjoy life for as long as possible. She was fond of Mum and once or twice a year she arranged for them to go to the theatre in the city, which Mum really loved, and I remember her being so excited to be going out. They travelled into the city by taxi and had dinner at a restaurant with Hannah's friends before the show.

I was fascinated by Mrs Jones' ability to slice the thinnest slices of bread I have ever seen. Before slicing, she would butter the bread and then, with a large, very sharp bread knife, she sliced the bread so thin you could almost see through it. She would spread it with her home-made apricot jam and roll it up before giving it to us to eat outside. It was an absolute delight to me. I remember Mr Jones was often in the backyard tending his vegetables. As he weeded and hoed his vegetable garden he was often followed by a thrush that hopped along eating the grubs that were exposed in the soil. He called it Hoppy and he even talked to it, saying "there's a nice big fat slug," or something similar, which really fascinated me.

Mrs Moss lived further down the hill and before my father died she did housework for us. Naturally, that had to stop when my mother became a widow. Mrs Moss was a tiny woman. Small and very thin, she seemed to run everywhere. I remember her hurrying up the hill towards Puckle Street to do her shopping and very soon after she would be hurrying back again. She was a widow and every month she would hop on the train and go to her husband's grave at Fawkner Cemetery. Following her visit to the cemetery, she often called in to see Mum for a cup of tea and a chat, and she was always upset. I remember Mum saying to her, "Win, I don't know why you keep doing it to yourself."

"Why don't you come with me?" Win answered.

Mum said she would never go to my father's grave because she didn't want to be upset like her friend.

Kindergarten

When I was four years old, I went to kindergarten which was held in a building belonging to the church we went to. I remember that I liked kinder, but it was very different from the kinder of today. When we arrived, we sat on little chairs in a circle and the teacher, Miss Peel, would play the piano for us to sing along to. I can still remember some of those songs I learned at kinder: Mrs Snail, Mr Frog and My Big Umbrella. I still remember the words. When we were permitted to play, there was a clear difference in the toys we were expected to play with. The boys were encouraged to go outside and play with cars and trucks and the girls were urged to play inside in the little playhouse corner. I remember Miss Peel telling one boy to leave the playhouse and go outside. Girls were allowed to play in the sandpit but it was not encouraged; the teacher preferred us to play with dolls and push prams. When we went back inside, we were given a piece of fruit and a glass of milk, then there would be more singing or a story and a prayer before we went home. Not a lot of free play. It was more structured, but we enjoyed it all the same. At Christmas time, we sang carols for the parents and I distinctly remember that when we sang Silent Night we did not sing 'yon virgin' but 'yon maiden.' I only remember this because I had already learnt the song elsewhere. How silly, they were only words, but it was 1951 and the teacher was a spinster. Still you can't trick children.

School 1

I can vividly remember my first day at school in prep when quite a few children cried long and loud. One boy, Robert Potts, cried the loudest and he had two green candles of snot running down from both nostrils to his open mouth. Another boy who cried had a wobbly head, which was supported by a metal frame fitted to his torso. I didn't cry. I was okay. I had been to kinder and, for some reason unknown to me I wasn't worried about being separated from my mother as Robert Potts and the wobbly-head boy were. I didn't even cry when I was made to sit outside the door as punishment for talking too much. The head teacher came along to ask why I was sitting outside the class room. I nervously explained that I had been telling someone about the Easter Bunny. She growled at me and said she would be keeping an eye on me and that the Easter Bunny might not come to children like me who talk too much. I was five years old and the Easter Bunny did come. Primary school was a fairly ordinary time for me, particularly after my father died when I was seven years old and in grade two.

In Grade 1, our teacher was Mrs Bear. She wore a fur coat when it was cold and we all thought she was aptly named. Poor wobbly-head boy brought a toy gun to school one day and showed it to the Mrs Bear who pushed the toy aside and said that she hated guns and his parents should be ashamed of themselves for allowing him to have a gun. This was in the early fifties and the war was still very real to adults, but it was the first time I had heard anyone saying anything against guns. Mind you, I agree with Mrs Bear and adopted the same attitude with my own children. All the same, she could have been a bit kinder to poor wobbly-head boy, who cried because he did not understand what was wrong with the gun.

When I was in Grade 2, a girl called Sandra stole about one hundred of my swap cards. I told Mum and she said to tell the teacher, who instructed the girl to go home and bring all of her swap cards back to school. She returned with about twenty cards and said that was all she had. That was the end of it and I don't expect the teachers cared one way or the other, but I was not happy. A year later, I found a bundle of swap cards dropped in the girls' shelter shed and when I looked at them, I thought they looked like the ones that were stolen from me. They probably were my cards because they belonged to Sandra; someone told her that I had picked up her swap cards, which I did, but in my mind, they were mine. I was made to stand up in front of the whole grade and be chastised. Naturally I cried bitterly and no one believed they were the same cards stolen from me previously. What lesson did I learn from that? I think I learned that one pile of swap cards looks pretty much like any other pile of cards and life is not always fair.

I had bought the swap cards with my pocket money, which my father gave to me every week. I had to do a few chores to earn two shillings, such as clean my room every Saturday and clean my school shoes. It was worth the effort and I realised how good it was to have money to spend, because once Dad died it stopped. There was a menswear shop nearby and I knew the man who owned it: he was a neighbour of ours. He had a broad smiley face and always wore an eye-catching bow tie, which I admired. I decided to buy a bow tie for my father when it was his birthday, so I went to the shop with all the money I had saved up and bought a very attractive blue and red one. It must have cost me at least a pound. When I gave it to Dad, he seemed to like it, but Mum took it back and changed it for something else. I can't remember what it was. On another occasion when I was still receiving pocket money, I spent quite a bit on a box of beautiful embroidered handkerchiefs for my mother. She never used them as she had plenty of handkerchiefs, but she kept them along with another box very similar to the one I bought and now I have them both.

When my baby brother was just a few months old I bought him a little teddy bear. It was about ten centimetres high and had a dark blue ribbon tied around its neck. I gave it to the baby who sucked on the ribbon, turning his mouth blue and almost choking him. Mum pulled the ribbon out of the baby's mouth and put the teddy bear aside until he was older.

When I was nine or ten, I had a friend called Janice who I had a lot of fun with and although she always wanted things her way, most of the time I went along with her. There were a large number of Italian migrants at our school and naturally they spoke to each other in Italian. Janice and I sometimes pretended to be Italian and would walk past people yabbering nonsense at the top of our voices. Pretty silly really. Janice had the best playhouse of anyone I have ever known. It was actually a sunroom, which ran down the western side of the house. She had beds, cupboards, a table and chairs—all child size—and so much fun for little girls to play with. Her brother bred pigeons and Janice sometimes took the pigeon eggs and mixed them with flour and sugar from her little play canisters. She told me and others that we could only play in her playhouse if we ate some of the mixture. I refused and went home. The next time I went there she made a little girl eat the mixture, which by now was not fit to be eaten and it made her sick. She had the runs. The little girl's mother came over to Janice's place to speak to her mother about it but Janice lied and said I had made the little girl eat it. They believed her and I went home crying to Mum who did believe me, and I was forbidden to go to Janice's place again. We did become friends again but that is pretty much the type of relationship we had.

Next door to Janice lived Angela, an only child who had everything that any child could possibly want and more. She was a plump girl with frizzy hair and big red chubby cheeks and she giggled a lot. We were playing together one day when she needed to go to the toilet. She took the only tennis ball we had and one tennis racquet with her. I remember Janice and me standing outside the toilet urging her to hurry up so that we could get on with our game.

"Come on, hurry up," said Janice. "What are you doing? You're taking too long."

"Look at this," yelled Angela, as she flung open the door.

There she was sitting on the outside toilet with her pink underpants around her plump little ankles holding something in her hand for us to see.

"I'm making a poo sandwich," giggled Angela, and she held out a large turd sandwiched between two pieces of toilet paper. She put one hand over the upper piece of toilet paper and squashed it.

"Oh, yuk!" we chorused. "That's disgusting!"

This made Angela cry. She cried because we didn't like her poo sandwich. She pulled up her pants, grabbed both tennis racquets and ran home yelling. And she didn't even pull the chain to flush the toilet. That was the last time she played with us, so after that we had to play games suitable for two but not tennis, because we had no racquets.

In Grade 5, Miss Brown was my teacher. To me, at ten years of age, she seemed as old as the hills and as cross as a bear. She rarely smiled and smacked us with a ruler if we played up. Miss Brown was very religious and some mornings she would preach to us about God and Jesus, heaven and hell, good and bad and various other biblical things. This preaching would go on until morning recess, and when we returned after running around outside for fifteen minutes, we had to do maths until lunchtime. I didn't mind listening to all her Bible stories in the beginning because I could daydream or listen, whichever I chose on the day, but I soon realised that if we were subjected to a religious hour, we would get more than an hour of maths to follow morning recess. I didn't like her. She was too strict and unbending and sometimes seemed cruel.

One day, Miss Brown caught Robert Potts picking his nose and eating it during one of her preaching episodes and got really angry with him.

"Do you think Jesus would like a boy who picks his nose?" she yelled at him.

"No," said Robert.

"Come here to me and put out your hand."

Robert went to the front of the class and held out his hand. It was whacked with a ruler and he returned to his seat mumbling something that sounded like, "Witch." She had been preaching to us that Jesus loved children and that he had said, "Suffer the little children to come unto me."

Is that why she made us suffer?

Wobbly-head boy, whose name was John, found a pencil sharpener on the floor and put it in his pocket. My friend Janice had dropped it and told Miss Brown that someone had stolen her pencil sharpener.

"Who has the pencil sharpener or who knows where the pencil sharpener is?" she roared.

"John has it," replied Sandra.

"Empty your pockets, John."

Poor John, who was not given a chance to defend himself, tried to say that he had just picked it up and was not going to keep it. Miss Brown would not listen and ordered him to come out the front to be whacked with the ruler.

"Jesus does not like boys who steal," she said, as she whacked him across his palm. "Thieves will never get into heaven."

I felt very sorry for him as he cried his way back to his desk, head wobbling from side to side.

One day when I went to church with Mum, I was surprised to see Miss Brown sitting in the pew in front of us with her friend Miss Sweet. It turned out they had decided to change churches because they heard we had a new minister, Mr Larkins, and that he was more their type of preacher.

"Fire and brimstone," I heard someone say.

So that meant I had to see her at school five days a week, at church on Sunday and at any social events held at the church.

Whenever there was a social event, it would be followed by a supper of sandwiches and cakes that the women from the congregation made to accompany a cup of tea for the adults or a cup of cordial for the children. At one of these events, I saw Miss Sweet standing very close to the table looking at a plate of cupcakes.

Thinking no one was looking, she quickly picked up the plate and emptied the cakes into her large handbag. Miss Brown was on the other side of the table watching her but she did not bat an eyelid. I thought she must have decided to say something to her friend when they were alone, but no, at every social event with cakes the same thing happened. I pondered over this and realised that Miss Brown was very selective when it came to making an example of people who stole. That is, children must not steal but old ladies can.

Miss Brown was only human and she obviously had boogies in her nose just like the rest of us. I know this because I saw her pick her nose. She didn't eat it, just looked at it and wiped it on her skirt. What did I learn from this? I learnt that when you are a kid, you have to be sneaky if you want to do certain things like pick your nose or pocket something that is not yours. But if you are an old lady, you can do whatever you like.

Bayswater

In the winter of 1957, my mother went away somewhere to have a rest. She had been very sad and depressed since my father died and it all got too much for her. My brothers and I were farmed out to various relatives for the duration. I have never found out how long we were apart, but it seemed like months to me. I went to stay with my uncle and aunt who lived on a poultry farm in Bayswater, which was in the bush in those days, and I really liked many things about it. My cousin, who was the same age as me, was very different from me, probably because she was an only child and quite smart. We walked to school together each morning along a road flanked by gum trees teeming with noisy birds. It was a very small school, which I think had only two classrooms and two teachers. After school, we sometimes walked home through a paddock where a small herd of cows grazed. One day, one of the cows chased me. I was really frightened and ran towards the fence where my little finger got stuck on the barbed wire. It tore my skirt and my finger and I cried for my mother who, I had by now heard, was having a nervous breakdown. Another day, when I was allowed to ride my cousin's pony, she instructed me on how to put the saddle on the pony. I must not have been listening properly because I ended up hanging on tight upside down looking through the pony's legs as it trotted back home. I didn't bother to try again.

I enjoyed some of my stay with this family because my cousin had lots of books and I loved to read. Also, she was learning the piano and gave me some lessons which I picked up easily. We had picnics in the paddocks and went out at night to look at nocturnal animals but I was scared of the dark and scared of what was under the bed. When it was time for bed, I would first stand at the doorway and then run like hell to get on top of the bed before the monster beneath got me. Sometimes I was even too scared to take off my dressing gown. I can't remember why though. I heard my uncle say to my aunt, "I think she is scared stiff, the poor thing."

He was correct and they were very kind to me.

While staying on the poultry farm, I liked to collect the eggs if my aunt asked me to help. I loved the different types of chickens and the warmth of the newly-laid eggs. I even enjoyed the sound of roosters crowing in the morning. The thing I loved the most was when the family allowed clucky hens to sit on their eggs and hatch adorable little fluffy chicks.

Eventually it was time for me to go home, and my aunt drove me to my grandparents' home in Elwood to meet my mother. I had missed her so much and was so pleased to see her standing in Grandma's lounge room. I ran to her and called out, "Mummy," throwing my arms around her waist. She pushed me away and told me to go outside. I walked outside and wandered around in the old tennis court that had been turned into a large garden. I watched the red and black harlequin bugs walking around, joined together, and wished I had a close friend I could be joined to.

School 2

We went home and I returned to my school and Miss Brown, but alas, my friend Janice was nowhere to be seen. No one thought to tell me that she had left the school and the neighbourhood. I had to ask numerous people until I found someone who knew.

"They had to leave suddenly," I was told. "Don't know why."

That was all I heard.

I had one more year at primary school and then I began secondary school. There were three co-ed schools I could have gone to but I chose the all-girls' school because I didn't like boys. No one advised me on which school I should go to and no one asked me anything about my choice of school. The school I had chosen was good but it was the most difficult to get to. I had to walk a mile to catch a tram and it was a fifteen-minute ride on the tram. The others were all much closer; there was a bus around the corner to one school and the other would have been a ten-minute train ride and we lived very close to the train station.

The family across the road who owned the delicatessen had three girls and when I began secondary school, I attended the same school as two of them. While I walked the mile to catch the tram, the girls across the road were driven by their mother in their big green and white car and they always passed me running down Puckle Street to the tram stop. I was always running late, but they never stopped to give me a lift and I could usually see one of the girls laughing at me as they sped past. I think that was very mean; they knew my situation and they knew we were having a difficult time. My mother was only just coping with four children on her own and sometimes she was very depressed and struggled to get out of bed in the morning. This in turn made it rather difficult for me in the morning. I would never do anything like that to a child. Even if I didn't like the child, I would not be unkind. I know I have instilled this into my own four children.

Mum did struggle at times and a lot of things did not get done or could have been done better. My brothers and I just got on with it and I don't remember any of us complaining. That was our lot.

An example of this is my cookery uniform. During the first year at secondary school, we had sewing lessons in which we each made an apron and cap to be worn when we took part in cooking lessons the following year.

One whole morning was devoted to cooking a three-course meal which we ate for lunch on that day and it was expected that our apron would be spotless before we began cooking. To cut a long story short, after the cookery morning I almost always shoved my apron into my locker and forgot about it until the following week when we had a cooking lesson. I would drag it out and put it on feeling a bit ashamed that it looked so creased and dirty, but I honestly never seemed to remember to take it home. Our teacher checked the aprons and gave us a mark out of ten. Most of the girls got a seven or an eight. Joyce always got a ten. Mind you, it was their mothers who washed and starched the aprons. I always got one or two. I suppose she had to give me a mark for actually having it on because those who didn't have their apron got zero. I enjoyed the cookery lessons and took it very seriously, taking some of the recipes home for the family. Mum and I would often cook together on the weekend, making cakes and biscuits to put in our lunch boxes during the week. I was very silly once and got very sick because I ate almost half of the uncooked cake batter straight out of the mixing bowl. As I vomited, Mum said, "I thought it should have been a bigger cake. Well, you've had your share."

On my first day of secondary school, a girl called Hilda came up to me and put her arms around my shoulders.

"What's your name?" she asked.

"Margaret," I replied with surprise. I was not used to this instant friendship, quite the opposite actually.

We became friends and joined up with several other girls who had gone to primary school with her. Hilda's home was a few miles away from the school and my home was much further along the tram line. She invited me to her place after school sometimes and I met her mother who, like mine, was quite old-fashioned. Hilda's mother always wore a hairnet over her permed hair so she looked like she was wearing a helmet.

"Why does your mother wear that thing on her head?" I asked Hilda.

"To keep her hair in place because my old woman is stuck in the olden days."

I had never heard anyone refer to their mother as 'my old woman' and when I told Hilda this she said, "Well, that's what she is and my father is 'the old man' and I don't like him."

I told her she was lucky to have a father and that mine had died.

"Wish mine would die," was her stern retort.

I didn't delve into why she did not like her father.

One time Hilda was away from school for several days so I hopped off the tram at her stop and called in to see her after school. She was in bed with a nasty cold and had a further week off school. Every night on the way home from school I called in to see her, which meant I was late home and was growled at by my mother. The next week she was back at school and I was sick as I had caught her cold, but did she come to see me? No. Not once. When I finally went back to school, I let her know that she was unfair and she apologised. She was the baby of the family and greatly indulged by her mother. I don't think she ever thought about anyone but herself. As soon as Hilda was old enough to leave school she did, and began work as a hairdressing apprentice. After that we were no longer friends. It seems that I was just a schoolgirl and she was more sophisticated than me. I went to the salon where she worked to have my hair done once and she barely spoke to me, but did talk about me and my hair as if I were not there. Anyway, the reason I mention Hilda is because her boss Jan told me something really funny about her. They went out together one night and got talking to a couple of young university students who they had a drink with.

Hilda said to the young man next to her, "What are you studying?"

"Pharmacy," he replied.

"Where is your farm?" Hilda asked.

According to Jan, the two men laughed so much they couldn't talk and soon got up and went away.

Maybe Hilda should have stayed at school a bit longer.

Christmas and Birthdays

On Christmas Day one year, my poor mother was so depressed that she couldn't get out of bed. She lay in bed with the covers pulled up over her head and gave instructions to my older brother on how to cook a roast for lunch. He was about twelve and I was about to turn ten. I set the table and kept an eye on the youngest boys who, fortunately, had some new toys for Christmas and were occupied. Mum eventually got out of bed in the early afternoon and we sat down in the dining room together. We were all a bit subdued as you can imagine, but we didn't say anything to upset Mum who had tears in her eyes. We didn't have Christmas pudding because that needed to be boiled for hours in the morning. Instead, we had tinned peaches with ice cream, which was fine. I don't remember much more about that day or what I received for Christmas, but I do remember my next birthday. My birthday is on January third and was often forgotten, being so close to Christmas. Mum continued to have difficulty getting out of bed and on the morning of my birthday I waited patiently for her to get up and give me a present. It was well into the afternoon when I could stand it no longer, so I went to her bedside to remind her that it was my birthday.

She answered, "Over on the dressing table there is a piece of material, I was going to make a dress for you with it."

I pulled open the brown paper to see the material, which was yellow with little coloured animals on it. It was a long time before I wore a dress made out of that piece of material.

Birthdays close to Christmas are often overlooked or downplayed because Christmas is such an expensive time and many presents are exchanged, but it is still important to the child whose birthday it is. I never had "Happy Birthday" sung to me at school or Sunday School and I felt I was missing out. At our weekly assembly at school, the head teacher would call out the names of people who'd had a birthday in that week and they went out the front and received a boiled sweet from a large jar. Sometimes she would say, "Is there anyone I have missed?"

This was my chance to get a boiled sweet, which I felt was my right. So I stood up and went out the front. She was surprised to see me but allowed me to have a sweet from the jar. Later that day, I was called to her office and questioned about why I had lied about my birthday. At first, I said it was my birthday but then I could see that she knew better, so I tried to explain that I never had a birthday during the school terms and I thought I missed out.

She listened to me and said, "You are quite right, and I will fix that. From now on we will call out the children who have had birthdays during the holidays."

From then on, at the first school assembly after the holidays, all the children who had celebrated a birthday were called up to the front to receive a boiled sweet from the head teacher's jar. I was quite proud of myself.

One birthday when I was about nine and before Mum had the nervous breakdown is very memorable. My mother's sister lived almost in the city, very close to the Shrine of Remembrance and the

Botanic Gardens in Melbourne. There were four boy cousins and a girl called Kate. We arrived at our aunt's place laden with baskets of food for a picnic in the Botanic Gardens. We all walked over, past the Shrine and into the beautiful gardens. We found a suitable grassy area under a tree near the lake where we could feed the ducks and swans. The boys spent a lot of time trying to catch long slithering eels which swam close to the surface of the water. When they managed to catch one, they put it on the grass and it quickly slid back into the water. We all rolled down the grassy hills, laughing as we bumped into each other. Mum made some of her famous pies: sausage, tomato, egg and bacon. We loved these pies. There was a birthday cake with candles for me. It was a great day until my very young brother, who was about two years old, stepped into the lake. Fortunately, my oldest cousin saw him slip under the water and grabbed him by the arm and pulled him out, saving his life. Mum cried. My brother cried. I didn't cry but I did have quite a few nightmares about the incident for months and months.

The City

After my father died, Mum had to go into the city every fortnight to receive a payment from the company my father had worked for. I don't know why they couldn't have done it any other way (such as sending her a cheque) but they didn't. We became very familiar with Mr Spencer who would hand Mum three green pound notes, ask how we all were and walk us to the door. When we were with her, she would take us to an hour show in one of the basement picture theatres. An hour show obviously went for an hour and consisted of a newsreel, two cartoons and a short documentary. It just kept repeating, hour after hour, all day long. Sometimes Mum went to sleep and we saw everything twice. If we went out for lunch in the city it was at Coles Cafeteria, which was a real treat. I usually had mixed triangular sandwiches and red jelly and cream. Mum always had a pot of tea and a fruit scone. We walked back to the Flinders Street railway station and caught a train home. That was something we all loved to do during the school holidays.

If Mum went during school hours, she sometimes brought home pies and pasties or a bag of mixed chocolates, which we really loved. When the pastries were heated up, she would cut them in half and we'd have two halves covered in tomato sauce. During the Christmas school holidays there was always a pantomime showing in one of the city theatres. We were lucky enough to be taken to some of these plays and they were amazingly colourful and funny: lots of singing, dancing and clapping in time to the music with the usual villain hiding in an obvious place. The children were encouraged to yell out where he was hiding. It was great fun. There were usually a couple of men dressed as funny old women and the lead man was played by a young woman, as is traditional in pantomime.

We went to the zoo about once a year and I can remember the small cages some of the poor animals were kept in, and how they walked up and down backwards and forwards all day. It is so much more humane now but we loved the zoo. There was an elephant which took people for a ride around a well-worn dusty circular track. A long bench seat was strapped on either side of the elephant where about six children could sit with a long belt around them all. With all of the circles she did, the poor elephant must have walked a million miles.

Mum also took us to the Museum which was also the art gallery and public library. The building is in Swanston Street and is now only the State Library, and has been restored to its former magnificence. I remember my brothers loved to look at the machinery inside glass cases. There were buttons to push that caused the machines to begin working, and we could see how the mechanics worked. One area contained dioramas behind glass, showing wild animals in their natural habitats. I can only remember the emus and kangaroos. Inside a small glass cabinet there was a tiger that had been cut in two and the front of its body was posed walking through long grass. It both fascinated and horrified me. I wondered why it had been cut in two and where the other half was. I still wonder. Mum liked to view the paintings in the gallery and I remember The Pioneers and

Shearing the Rams; two paintings that I still love. Because it was a small gallery, there were not many paintings on display, and it is only since our new galleries have been opened that we have been able to see so much of the art that rarely saw the light of day.

Once when we were with Mum in the city, we walked across Princes Bridge and a man who was nearby said to Mum, "Look at all the money down there."

We all stopped to look down onto the pylons where an enormous number of coins had been thrown. When we finished trying to guess how much money was down there, we turned and Mum discovered someone had stolen her purse from her handbag lying open on the pram. Luckily, Mum had put the three one-pound notes into a zipped pocket in her bag so the thief only got the loose change in the purse.

Horse and Cart

In the fifties, many services were still done by tradesmen travelling in a cart pulled by a horse. The baker had an attractive chestnut horse which pulled a beautiful green cart decorated with black and gold writing. It had double doors at the back where he kept the bread. He wore a large boot on his deformed foot and limped from the front of the cart to the back, where he opened the doors to take out a huge cane basket full of freshly baked bread. With the basket over his arm, he walked towards the gates of the houses where women and children were waiting to purchase the loaves. Next, he returned the basket to the back of the cart, pulled himself up to his seat and flicked the reins for the horse to proceed up the hill.

A milkman delivered milk into a billycan which was kept in a special little cupboard at the side of the house. He came early in the morning before the sun came up and usually one of the children would collect the billycan to take it inside. I spilt the whole lot one morning so there was no milk for breakfast that day. Sometime later in the fifties, milk was delivered in milk bottles. The bottles had silver tops and the first few centimetres on top of the milk was cream, which you could pour off and have as a special treat, or you could shake the bottle and mix the cream into the milk. Sometimes birds would get to the bottles of milk and dig a hole in the silver top to get a drink. When this happened, we had to boil the milk before using it. The silver milk bottle tops were collected and used for art and craft, mostly to make bells at Christmas time or chains to hang up as decoration.

Down the back of the properties were cobble-stone laneways where we left our rubbish bins, which were collected by a man driving an open cart, pulled by an enormous draught horse. That was a smelly job. The man walked down the lane picking up the bins and emptying them into the cart, and the horse walked on at a steady pace, never too fast or too slow.

Another horse-and-cart pair was the Bottle-O, who also drove an open cart, which he steered around the streets calling out at the top of his voice, "Bottle-O, Bottle-O!"

Some of my friends knew where he lived and one day I went with them to the back gate of his property with an old pram. We filled up the pram with the Bottle-O's bottles, pushed the pram to the front door, sold them back to the Bottle-O then went to the milk bar and bought an ice cream each. Mum saw us walking back home and asked me where I had got the ice cream. When I told her, she was so angry she smacked me and grabbed what was left of my ice cream, throwing it in the gutter. As quick as a wink, a hungry-looking dog rushed over and devoured it.

The house where the Bottle-O lived was a magnificent grey Italianate building that stood on a large block of land. This beautiful piece of architecture was demolished to make way for a local hospital; such a shame, but there were a lot of wonderful buildings pulled down in those days when many people did not like anything old.

The working horses that pulled the carts were a great source of manure for our gardens, and whenever a horse pooed there would be a rush by the mothers or their children to hurry out and collect the droppings with an old brush and shovel. It was always a race to see who would get there first. One of our neighbours had four sons who were always waiting at the gate and they usually got it and made fun of those who didn't. I never joined in this game but my brothers did.

Cousins

After Mum had her nervous breakdown, one of my cousins came to stay with us. I think it must have been decided by Mum's sisters because they always bossed Mum around. During the year after my father died, both the aunts arrived to help Mum clean up the house. They cleaned out Dad's wardrobe and burnt Mum's wedding dress, which made her cry. Poor Mum. She managed to save the artificial violets that had decorated the hat she had worn for her wedding day. I still have the violets.

One of the aunts decided it would be a good idea for her son to come and stay with us to give Mum some support. He was about to start work in the city so it was convenient for him. He was bossy and made a roster for us to help around the house, but he never did anything to help Mum.

The first night he stayed at our place he molested me. I remember it clearly. I was sitting up in my bed reading one of my favourite books when he came into my room. He pretended he was going to read to me but he put his hand under the bedclothes and into my pyjamas and grabbed my vulva. I pushed his hand away and he said to me, "You like it don't you?"

"No," I said.

Then he left the room. I still remember the book I was reading.

I still have it. It has an orange cover and contains myths, fables and fairy tales.

On another occasion he came into the bathroom when I was having a bath and said to me, "you look nice."

I covered myself with my face washer. I told Mum and she said I was being silly, but it never happened again. I don't know if he came to his senses or if Mum said something to him. I made myself forget the incidents for years and years but it did give me a few problems which I won't go into.

I don't remember how long he stayed at our place but he left at some stage and returned a few years later when I was about thirteen. He rode a motorbike. He had a girlfriend who was very good to me and I liked her very much. I pretended that she was my big sister. She was a hairdresser and she did my hair sometimes and helped me with my dressmaking. They got married and, as I write this, they are still together.

I did not tell my cousin's wife about his molesting me until I was in my sixties and the reason for remembering and telling her has no real connection to the molestation. In the front room of the house where I lived as a child, there was a room where antique furniture was stored. It was in this room that Mum cleared a space for my cousin's bed. As well as the Chinese antiques, there were pictures hanging on the walls. These pictures were sepia lithographs of pastoral scenes and naked women lying around in the sunshine. They had belonged to my grandparents, as had the Chinese antiques—a strange combination. I remember the pictures vividly; one in particular, a pastoral scene of a group of men and women dressed in early nineteenth century clothes holding their horses as they gathered to talk at garden steps.

When my cousin left our house, so did these pictures. I asked

Mum why they had gone with my cousin and she brushed me off without an explanation.

A few years ago, when I asked my cousin where they all were, he let it slip that they were valuable and he had spent money having them reframed and restored where needed, and then sold them for a substantial profit. Some were given to other members of his family. When my daughter was married, she was given one of the unrestored pictures of a cat with kittens and told it was back in the family now where it belonged. This made me angry and brought up the memory of the pictures disappearing and the molestation long ago. My cousin kept at least two of the pictures for himself. One is the picture of the group with the horses which I had seen hanging in his home. When I confronted him and asked him why he had taken them all from our house so long ago, he replied that my mother had given them to him and that they were not worth much. This was a contradiction of what he told me previously about them being valuable. That my mother said, "take them," is probably true, because I know that she was chronically depressed and always taking the easy way out. Not wanting any conflict, she would very easily have given in to badgering. I have seen her do this several times because it was easier than arguing or worrying. My cousin said the pictures had been stored in the shed and had fallen onto his motorbike, causing damage, but this is not true. Some of them may have been stored in the shed but they were secure, as were many other things stored in the rafters. He spent a lot of time in the shed with his friend and my older brother tinkering with their motorbikes, so he could easily have found them.

Later, I asked my mother if she could remember giving the pictures to him and she replied, "Yes. I got sick of him going on and on about what I was going to do with them so I said just take the damn things."

This was typical of Mum.

I told my cousin the pictures should never have left the house and that I wanted the picture I have described. He told me that I had received plenty of things from my mother and I should be grateful, which is ridiculous. She was my mother, not his. When I confronted his wife with the whole story, she told me she would give me the picture when my cousin died. This might seem petty to some people but to me those things, which had belonged to my grandparents and in turn my mother, should have remained in the house for my brothers and I. My cousin would not have wanted them if they were not valuable and unusual.

My sweet gentle cat, Brigitte, was terrorised by this cousin who had a nasty streak in his nature. He thought it was funny to put a tight elastic band around the cat's middle which eventually caused her to become temporarily paralysed and unable to walk. Once when this happened, I could hear her crying and went to investigate, finding her trying to drag herself away from him. I rescued her and tried to keep her out of his sight. Another time he soaked a rag with petrol and wiped it onto the cat's bottom. It stung her and she ran screaming all over the back yard, trying to get away from the stinging. I rescued her again and had to give her a bath and put oil on her poor little sore bottom. He was not a very nice person and neither was his older brother, who I will call Jack.

When I was about forty, I was told that my cousin Jack had molested his daughter and terrorised his family for many years. This caused untold damage to his children and an enormous rift in the family. Jack and his wife had always given the impression they were perfect parents, with wonderful children, but it was all a lie. His eldest daughter and I have become close friends and she has told me about the terrible things that were inflicted on them by Jack. He was a monster and so were other members of that family. When Mum's sister was giving birth to one of her many children she needed my mother to look after the other little ones. Mum stayed and cared for the children all day when her sister was in hospital and at night her brother-in-law pestered her and attempted to get into bed with her. Mum's trick was to take the other children to bed with her and to push a dressing table up against the door each night.

My cousin Kate, sister of these brothers, unfortunately killed herself when she was in her early thirties. We will never know what dreadful things were done to her by her father and perhaps her brothers. Kate was a nurse and was helping to care for a sick, wealthy, well-known Melbourne businessman in his home. One Saturday afternoon, Mum was at our neighbour's place when the news came on the television. Mum almost fell off her chair when the image of a young bride emerging from a church on the arm of a very elderly man appeared on the television screen. It was my cousin Kate, Mum's niece, and she knew nothing about the marriage. Mum raced home in tears and went next door to use their phone to speak to her sister and brother-in-law. Apparently, they had given their blessing to this ridiculous marriage. The marriage did not last long and Kate was admitted to a psychiatric hospital for some time. Following discharge from the hospital, she went to her parents' home, lay down in the back garden, put her father's gun in her mouth and pulled the trigger.

Kate was a lovely girl. I remember her coming to stay when she was about fourteen years old, probably to get away from some abuse at home. She took my brothers and I to the Royal Melbourne Show and I had my first experience in the scary ghost train, which I hated. I saw her twice after she was married. Once when I was going to the beach with a boyfriend and Mum asked me to drop off something to Kate, who lived with her husband in the beachside suburb of Brighton. She seemed happy to see me but gave the impression of excessive protection by hovering over the old man (her husband) who was reclining on a chaise longue in the living room. When we left, my boyfriend said, "Sex would be like trying to put a marshmallow into a money box."

The last time I saw Kate was in Adelaide when I was on holiday with a friend. We met up with her for lunch. Towards the end of the meal Kate stood up and, without saying anything, paid for the three of us and left without saying goodbye. It was not long after that day that she killed herself. Poor Kate. What on earth happened to her to cause such unhappiness and unusual behaviour?

Dreams

After my father's death I frequently had awful nightmares, which is quite normal after such a traumatic event. Two dreams have remained in my memory all my life. The first was about my mother. I dreamt I was in the home of a neighbour with various people I knew. Mum was standing at a large table making sandwiches, along with a group of women. She was looking at me and had tears running down her cheeks. She couldn't reach me on the other side of the table and I wanted to get out of the house, but there was a fire preventing my escape at the back door and a pride of lions prowling at the front door. After looking to Mum for help and not getting any, I realised I had to take one of the exits so I chose the front door and the lions. I ran past them and raced up the street to our house. I tried to fly, but I kept falling to the footpath, eventually reaching the gate and safety. Years later, I realised that this dream was telling me that I was pretty much on my own.

The other dream I had more than once was where I was at the bottom of a deep dark pit. At the top, looking down and grinning at me, was my father sitting in his favourite chair. Deepening water was swirling around my feet and my father made no attempt to save me. Not long after the first time I had this dream, I was walking along the edge of the public swimming pool trying to find my brother when someone pushed me in. I couldn't swim and floundered about under the water until somebody pulled me out and put me on the side of the pool. I coughed and spluttered, then stood up and continued to look for my brother, who I didn't find. I walked all the way home on my own and on reaching home I told Mum that I had almost drowned. She did not seem to be worried. So began my fear of water and I never learned to swim, which caused me to project my anxiety onto my children who, in spite of that, can swim. I did have swimming lessons twice as an adult but I could only go to a certain stage. As soon as I had to swim in deep water, I gave up.

A few years later, it was at this swimming pool that I had my first romantic encounter. Wayne Fawkner was a good-looking young guy who many girls liked, and for some reason (which surprised me), he was attracted to me. It was a Saturday when he approached me and asked me to go to the movies with him that night. It was during the summer holidays and I would have just turned fourteen. He said he would meet me at the Moonee Ponds picture theatre. I didn't think I would be allowed to go but surprisingly Mum said I could if my older brother went also. My brother disappeared as soon as we turned the corner and went off with his friends. I met Wayne and we held hands during the film and on the way home we stopped in the middle of Puckle Street and kissed. It was a very nice kiss and I enjoyed quite a few more over the next month or so. When he split up with me, I was heartbroken and cried all day. Mum said I would get over it and I did.

Grade Four

Mr Golden was my teacher in Grade Four. He was okay. He had a sense of humour and he was not too strict. Sometimes he would ask us if we had anything to share or present to the class. I had always wanted to do something but my nervousness stopped me. One day, after rehearsing at home, I decided to stand up and recite a poem, which was from one of my favourite Ladybird books. It is a childish piece but I knew it word for word. With my head held high and in my best pronunciation, I recited As I Walked Up The Gravel Drive. The look on Mr Golden's face was one of astonishment and I was pleased to have given him a surprise. He asked me later where I had learned the poem and if I read very much at home, along with a few other questions. After that day, he treated me with a bit more attention, often requesting that I read out loud to the class. I must add, the class size was forty children or more so there was not much time for him to get to know all the children well or to know what they could or could not do. He concentrated more on the children who were badly behaved or who were good at sport. I informed him of my uncle, a well-known author who had been a war correspondent during WWII and this knowledge, along with a few photographs and a copy of one of his latest books, put me in the limelight for a week or two.

I'm not sure why, but at times we were required to go outside and partake in a session of folk dancing. The instructions and music were broadcast over a loudspeaker. Most of us didn't like the dancing because we did not want to hold hands with the opposite sex. We skipped up and down, dipping and diving under arches of joined arms, wishing it would soon end. In the spring some girls were chosen to take part in maypole dancing. I was never one of the chosen few but I would have liked to try. There were several maypoles and they each had twelve pretty pastel-shaded pieces of fabric hanging from the top of the pole. The girls who danced wore white dresses and floral wreaths in their hair and as they danced the correct steps, the fabric became woven into a very pretty design. It always looked really lovely and received cheers and lots of applause.

A school ball was held every second year in the Moonee Ponds Town Hall. Over a month or so we all learnt various ballroom dances such as the Barn Dance, the Pride of Erin and others, which I can't remember. It was a big deal and most of the girls were dressed in pretty, long flowing gowns. I wore a white floor-length dress that Mum made for me. I remember she took me to the hairdresser to have my hair done and I loved the way my curls bounced up and down if I jumped. There was one dance called Hands Knees and Bumpsadaisy, where we bumped the hands of our partner, patted our own knees and turned around to bump the backside of our partner. A few of the boys tried really hard to knock the girls flying and some of them succeeded, and although they had been threatened with detention they did it anyway and swore it was accidental.

The School Fete

Just like today, primary schools held a school fete yearly or every second year. It was a big deal and we were dismissed at lunchtime on the day of the fete so that we could enjoy the games and rides and buy the bits and pieces of handicrafts or toys. There were always toffees in patty pans decorated with hundreds and thousands—great for the teeth and for removing fillings! I remember one year I had four shillings saved up to take to the fete and I took the money to school in a tiny purse. Somehow, I lost the purse and I walked around and around looking for it. I didn't find it (surprise, surprise). It so happened I had a sore arm from a recent fall and the more I looked for my purse the more my arm hurt. Someone was blowing a trumpet and every time I heard the trumpet my arm ached more. The sound of the trumpet seemed to intensify the pain. Finally, I saw Mum and I cried as I told her I had lost my money. She gave me a penny and so I bought a toffee and walked home alone, sucking on my only purchase.

Gerry the Dog

We had a dog called Gerry. He was a barrel of a dog with boundless energy. It was not uncommon for him to arrive home with a squawking chicken in his mouth. Unfortunately, sometimes the chicken lost its squawk as it was brought across the road to our back door. I'm not sure what was done with these dead chickens. I think he would have been better off living on a farm with cows or sheep that needed to be rounded up.

We had some friends who worked at a local pie factory and sometimes on the weekend they would bring us half a dozen pies. We enjoyed them in the beginning, but after a while, we had had enough of pies. Mum decided to give one or two of the pies to Gerry, who quickly gobbled them up. After a while, like us, even Gerry seemed to be over the pies. He didn't gobble them up but he still took them. When Mum was gardening she discovered that Gerry had been burying his pies with the odd bone, as dogs do. I am not sure why the pies stopped, but they did; however they kept turning up in the garden for a while.

Andrew

Most of the time I got on with my brothers, although the middle one would sometimes punch me in the stomach and wind me. I can't remember why, but I suppose I must have done something to upset him. One night, I upset my older brother Andrew when I sat in a chair that he liked to sit in to watch TV in the lounge room; he considered it his chair. I refused to move and we argued until he pulled me out of the chair and threw me on to the floor. I remember that I was hurt but, more to the point, I was really angry.

To get back at him, the next day when he was out, I found an old tin of green paint and a paintbrush in the shed. I went into his bedroom and stood on top of the cedar chest of drawers and painted 'Andrew is a bastard' high up on the wall. To get back at me, he brought various people from the church and neighbours in to have a look. I did not care and the words remained on the wall for years. My mother was not impressed in the beginning and she growled at me a few times, but she eventually just forgot about it.

One day when this same brother of mine was about ten, he decided to run away from home. Why? I can't remember, but he was not as brave as he pretended to be. We looked all over the place for him and were starting to worry until I discovered him up a tree in the back yard.

"Don't tell Mum I'm here," came a voice from the top of the cherry plum tree.

"Well, how are you going to live up there? How will you go to the toilet?"

"I'll just wee down the side of the tree and you can bring me food," he instructed. "Oh, and bring me a few comics please."

I found a small basket, tied a rope around the handle and, without Mum noticing, filled it with an apple, banana, a huge lump of cheese and biscuits. Taking the basket to the bottom of the tree, I began throwing the end of the rope skywards. It took many attempts for the rope to reach my brother. It did eventually and he began to eat, although it wasn't even lunchtime. These antics continued all day, interspersed with Mum's angry exclamations of, "Who hacked at the cheese!" and "I'm sure there were more biscuits in the cupboard."

Later, I heard her say to my younger brother, "What is Margaret doing out there? Why is she always popping into the back garden?"

I couldn't hear his reply. It began to get dark and my brother, who was still up in the tree, asked me what Mum was cooking for dinner. His favourite food was Mum's egg and bacon pie so I told him that was on the menu for tonight. It wasn't true but I said it anyway. It was my turn to set the table and I was not sure if I should set a place for my brother or not. I decided to set a place for him and Mum said I thought we would be one less tonight. I began to get worried because Mum did not seem to care that Andrew had run away. We sat down to eat. It was dark outside and then it began to rain, just lightly at first then it became a deluge, pelting down so heavily on the corrugated tin roof of the veranda that we could hardly hear each other speak. I looked at Mum, who did not seem concerned at first, but she kept glancing at the back door.

"Margaret, would you go out onto the veranda and call your brother please? He will be drenched," Mum said, not looking at me but grinning to herself. Suddenly, the back door was thrown open and my brother (looking like a drowned rat) burst into the kitchen. He was not happy. Actually, he was fighting back tears.

"Don't you care about me any more, Mum?"

"Certainly I care about you. I have known all day that you were quite safe up a tree in the back garden."

He had a hot shower and sat down for dinner. He gave me an angry look as he began to eat his least favourite meal: tripe fritters. We only ate the batter and put the tripe into our pockets to feed to the dog later.

Fires

I remember we had three fires, which could have burnt the house down; two were lit by my middle brother and one (I think) was an electrical fault. My brother was sitting on the potty in my parents' bedroom and as he sat, he opened a bedside cabinet and found some matches, which he began to strike. The contents of the cabinet were mainly books and papers, which he decided to light. The flames became large and frightening and he began to yell. My father, who was fortunately nearby in the bathroom, looked in and responded by shutting the door of the cabinet and removing it from the bedroom. The cabinet was put on the front veranda to cool down and a few weeks later, my father restored it. It remained in the bedroom to see many more years of use.

The second fire was in the bathroom and it seemed my parents were still careless with where they put matches. In our bathroom we had a gas water heater. Lighting it scared the living daylights out of me and I never felt comfortable doing it. As it required matches to light the gas, the matches were left nearby. My middle brother was playing in the bath one night when he decided to light a match and see how a towel would look as it burnt on the wall rail. I saw it and I can say it looked pretty scary as it began to ignite the timber wall lining. I yelled for Mum who pulled my brother from the bath and flicked the towel into the bath water. I think that was the last time any matches were left around the house. Dad restored the bathroom.

The third fire was in the laundry, which was fortunately outside at the end of the back veranda. We had been at the church, helping Mum who cleaned the church each week. We helped her dust the pews by sitting at one end and whizzing along to the other end to remove the dust. Sometimes, one of us would get up into the pulpit and pretend to be the minister giving a sermon. Mum didn't seem to mind. I think she liked our company. Once when we went to the church to clean on a different day, we encountered a church elder with one of the boys from the cricket club. They were in the minister's private room. When the elder saw Mum he ushered the boy out very quickly.

"I don't know what on earth he's doing here," said Mum.

Walking up the hill towards home, we saw a fire truck in our street, never dreaming it was at our place.

"Someone's house is on fire," said my middle brother.

"Hope it's not our house," I answered.

Well, it was our house, and our laundry was full of water where the firemen had squirted their hose to put out the fire. What a mess! For some reason, our pet goldfish had been put in the laundry and the bowl had cracked in the heat. There was about one centimetre of water remaining in the bowl but the fish somehow survived the incident. I took it inside and put it into a clean bowl of water and it lived on. Unfortunately, Dad was not alive then to restore the laundry so it remained in a charred condition for some time.

Those Pants

Andrew must have been about fourteen years old when Mum gave him the money to go into the city to buy himself a pair of jeans. He had never been allowed to do this before so he was pretty chuffed. With his mate Allen he caught an early train into the city on a Saturday morning on his first solo-shopping trip for clothes.

About 11am, Mum and I were hurrying to Puckle Street to do some shopping before the shops closed at twelve. We turned the corner into Holmes Road and approached the railway line. As we neared the train station, a red rattler arrived at the station and a handful of people alighted. Some of these people began to walk towards us and Mum said, "Will you look at that?"

"What?"

"Look what that boy is wearing."

"That boy is Andrew, Mum."

"My god! I'll kill him."

Andrew and Allen were standing in front of us now and both were grinning but Andrew's grin had a sheepish air about it. He was wearing a pair of bright aqua pants. Mum was so angry I thought she would burst.

"Go home," she said to Andrew. "Go home and take them off at once."

"I like them, Mum," he said.

"Well, I don't. Get out of my sight."

Mum boiled all weekend and the following Monday she took the pants back to the shop in the city to change them. The shop would not change them because Andrew had worn them home, so she took them to the dry cleaners to have them dyed. But they couldn't dye them because they were made of polished cotton, which wouldn't take dye. So Andrew had to wear them and they took ages and ages to wear out. They were a real talking point. Everyone in the area knew my brother as the boy in the aqua pants. I don't think even he liked them in the end. They were very bright.

Out at Night

Andrew wanted to go out on Saturday night but Mum wouldn't allow him to go unless it was a church function. She told him that when he was sixteen, he might be able to go out at night but not before. He was well and truly over boys' club and Bible studies so he had to employ a sneaky method to get out. It's nothing new, but it was new to my naive mother who would never have done some of the things we got up to.

Saturday night came around and Andrew asked if he could go out with his mates. Mum said no and that seemed to be the end of it. He got sulky and stormed off to bed early.

Several Saturday nights went by in exactly the same way, then on one particular Saturday night I went into his bedroom to get a book I wanted to read and discovered his bed was empty and the window ajar. I laughed to myself but decided to keep quiet and not tell Mum. I didn't know what he was doing when he went out but he was always there in the morning.

We were allowed to go to the swimming pool and the movies on Saturday afternoons at the Ascot Theatre, both within walking distance. At the swimming pool one weekend, a boy called Roger and his friend began to talk to my school friend Susan and me. I didn't think anything of it but at the picture theatre the next Saturday afternoon, Roger came and sat next to me and without a word put his arm around me. I didn't know what to do so I did nothing but at the interval, I moved to another seat. Roger came and sat next to me again and put his arm around me. This was not unusual for young teens. I think their mates egged on the boys and the theatre was dark. I was not really comfortable but I didn't tell him to go away. I don't know why. I suppose it was uncharted waters. As soon as the lights went on, I was out of there and walking towards home. My brother and his friend Allen caught up with me and began to tease me, which I didn't like at all.

"Ha! We saw you with that dingbat Roger," said Andrew.

"I've seen you sitting next to girls in the picture theatre," I replied

"Yeah, but you're too young."

"Leave me alone. I didn't ask him to sit next to me," I said.

"Well, why didn't you move?"

"I did, now leave me alone."

When we arrived home, Andrew told Mum about Roger sitting next to me and that he put his arm around my shoulders. Mum was not impressed. "Well, if I can't trust you to do the right thing and behave properly you will not be going to the pictures again and that's that."

It was no use arguing with her. She was really angry with me. That night Andrew began his usual Saturday evening request to go out with his friends and Mum, as usual, said no. He went to bed early and I sat in the living room with Mum and my other brothers.

"Mum, why does Andrew go to bed early on Saturday night?"

"I suppose he's tired."

"I don't think so," I said.

"What are you getting at?" asked Mum.

"Let's go and see if he is asleep," I said.

"Well, the light is off, he must be asleep."

I got up and went to his bedroom door, pulled it open, turned on the light and called out, "Come and have a look, Mum! You won't believe this."

Mum saw the open window. I watched as the penny dropped.

"How long have you known about this?" she asked.

"Just worked it out," I replied.

Mum was fuming. She rushed to the window and slammed it shut and locked it. Leaving the bedroom door slightly open, she returned to the living room and I'm sure I heard her swear. She stayed up until she heard the window rattling about 11pm, when she returned to the bedroom and stared at Andrew through the window.

That was the end of his early Saturday nights, and Mum said that he would not be allowed to go out at night with his friends until he was seventeen.

Valentines

When I was about thirteen or maybe fourteen, my friend Susan and I cunningly decided to play a St Valentine's Day trick on our brothers. Both of our brothers had left school and were into their second year as apprentices. The plan was to buy a St Valentine's card and each of us send it to the other brother without a name from the sender. A bit naughty I know, but it seemed like a good idea at the time. So, we sent the cards and the brothers received them. Neither brother said anything at first but eventually I overheard my brother telling his friend Allen about this hot girl who had sent him a card. This was my chance to enter into the conversation.

"How do you know who she is?" I asked.

"I see her when I'm riding up Park Street," he sneered at me.

"Oh. Okay, but it could be that fat ugly girl from church who is always making eyes at you."

"I don't think so because when I wave to this girl, she smiles at me."

"Are you going to stop and talk to her?" asked Allen.

"Yes, next time I see her I will."

I began to think this could go wrong; should I tell him or not? He never got to speak to her because she wasn't seen again on his ride to work and he was angry with himself for not stopping to speak to her when he had the chance. It all died down and then one day when he was being particularly nasty to me, I blurted out, "That hot girl didn't send you a card. It was my friend Susan."

"I don't believe you. Yeah, what's Susan like anyway?" said Andrew.

I thought it was about time I came clean with the whole thing, so I told him what Susan and I had done. He looked at me and I thought he was going to whack me but instead he began to laugh and laugh. When he stopped laughing, he said, "You little bitch."

More School

Most of my time at primary school is a blur. I was invisible for the most part, just one of the forgettable hordes of children, another brick in the wall. I've told you about the swap cards, Tommy the tap dancer, and my friend who made little children eat raw pigeon eggs mixed with flour and who once stuck chewing gum in my hair.

Secondary school was a totally different experience. I became one of the semi-popular girls and was even a school prefect. One of my friends left school at thirteen to have a baby. She was one of three. I was aware of who became a mother very early. There was another girl who was absent for about three months, and the rumour was that she had given birth to a baby, which had been adopted. Those poor girls were all victims of ignorance, naivete and one of nature's surprises. In spite of this, there were still girls of my age who had no knowledge of sex and reproduction. Some thought you could get pregnant from kissing and one girl thought a baby was born through the navel. No wonder so many girls got pregnant.

As we know, teenage girls can be very mean to each other. Two of my friends suddenly became nasty towards me. It happened overnight and I could not work out what I had done; probably nothing. One of them was really good looking and had a lot of influence over the other. Everything I said or did, they made fun of: the material my mother had chosen to use in sewing lessons, my hair, my scruffy school shoes, a hole in my navy stockings, and anything else they could pick on. After a while, I was over it and managed to ignore them and keep out of their way. The worst bullying I experienced was not from a schoolgirl but from an adult. I had to go to the dental hospital to have a tooth filled so I left school early and caught a tram into the city on my own. Reclining in the dentist's chair, I was waiting for the procedure to begin when a dentist and a dental student came and stood at my elevated feet.

The older man said to the student, "We often get little tarts like this in here."

The student did not answer and I like to think he did not think it was appropriate. It really hurt my feelings and I did not know what I had done to deserve such a comment, and I did not have the courage to defend myself.

I did not tell my mother, but she would not have done anything anyway.

When I was in year nine, our school had a social night with a local boys' school. It was a big deal and now that most of us liked boys, we all wanted to go. I made a new dress to wear out of blue and white checked fabric. It had a full skirt, puffed sleeves, a lace insert at the neck and was worn with a petticoat, which helped it to look very full. This was the fashion at the time. Mum was always at me to cut my nails and keep my hair pulled back. She said I could only go if I let her cut my nails and because I really wanted to go to the dance, I reluctantly agreed. I sat on a chair and instead of cutting my nails, she hacked off a long tress of my hair. She cut the other side to even it up and I became hysterical. I loved my hair. It was long, thick, healthy auburn hair and it was all on the floor. I cried and cried so much; I couldn't believe what she had done to me and I could not talk to her for ages afterwards. My grandfather was very cross with Mum for cutting my hair, although he did not know the story of how it happened. Anyway, I went to the social and I was swept off my feet by James the pianist who became my boyfriend. He drove me home in his blue Mini Minor and as we turned the first corner when leaving the boys' school, the car slid to the left, hit the curb and damaged the tyre. He seemed to enjoy himself as his band members watched him change the tyre, and then off we went. He was crazy about cars. I had thought that with short hair no one would look sideways at me.

James was much older than me and already an apprentice and driving a car. My mother began to get concerned. When Mum told me I was not to see James again because he was too old for me, I was heartbroken. I had, up until this point, had very little affection in my life and I didn't really have a great deal of self-confidence. I didn't feel loved so the affection I got from him was a new experience. I spent a lot of time at his place and became very fond of his parents and grandparents who lived next door to them.

At this time, I was having piano lessons one night a week after school, which I quite enjoyed. I really only wanted to play Für Elise, so that's what I was working towards. Not seeing James made me so unhappy and I realised the only way I could see him was to skip my piano lesson and meet him after school. So that's what I did. Unfortunately, the piano teacher contacted Mum and one of the ever-vigilant sticky-noses from the church saw me get into James' car and told Mum.

Mum was so angry with me that she came into the bathroom when I was washing my hands, baled me up in a corner and thrashed me with a rope. She was my mother and was supposed to love me, yet that was the way she treated me. It was really awful. I cried and cried and I know from that day onwards, the relationship between my mother and I changed for the worse. She didn't explain why I was not to see him. She just kept hitting me. I have had four children of my own and I have had to deal with similar things with my children, but never, ever, did I resort to that type of abuse. I don't think she knew what to do. I suppose that is what was done to her by her father. I don't know. It didn't stop me though. I was determined to keep seeing him and he was my boyfriend until I finished school. Mum just accepted it in the end. So much for the belting.

Mum did other silly things, which people these days will find ridiculous. I had a collection of pictures of pop singers stuck on my wardrobe doors and an almost life-sized picture of Cliff Richard on the back of my bedroom door. One day when I came home from school, they had all disappeared. When I asked Mum where they were, she said, "I put them out with the waste paper."

I was so angry I went outside and pulled up some of her plants and cut a rose bush off at the bottom. Another time when I was sick and away from school, one of my friends, Carol, came to see me and brought some love comics for me to read. They were harmless really but my mother thought they were dreadful and she burnt them all. When Carol asked for them back, I had to tell her what my mother had done. I was surprised at her answer.

"They belonged to my mother. She will be angry with me for lending them to you."

I told Mum they belonged to Carol's mother but she didn't believe me. I spent what pocket money I had saved to buy a few new love comics for Carol's mother.

Vanity

Mum made me a kilt when I was about twelve and I wore it for a couple of years. It was made from pure wool tartan, I'm not sure of the clan. One day, I decided to cut it up and make a straight skirt and a short-sleeved jacket. Naturally, Mum was not happy that I had cut up the kilt but when she saw what I made with it she was a bit forgiving. I made a mess of the sleeves and didn't have enough fabric to recut them, so it was sleeveless but it looked nice with a short-sleeved black jumper I owned. It was during the winter and on the school holidays that I had an appointment at the dental hospital in the city, a perfect opportunity to wear my new outfit and although it was cold, I wore it. As soon as I stepped outside and proceeded up the hill towards the train station, I began to feel the cold. In the train it was bearable but walking up Collins Street in the city, the wind was strong and freezing cold. I shivered all through the treatment and set off home chilled to the bone. Arriving home, I was met by Mum who said to me, "I bet you won't do that again. Comfort wins over vanity any time, don't you think?"

   I had to agree with her and I was always very careful not to be so silly again.

Mum's Traditional Cooking

Mum was not a very good cook for everyday food but for the traditional foods eaten at Easter and Christmas, she was excellent. Day to day, she burnt a lot of saucepans and there were always several hanging on the apricot tree outside the back door. They stayed there until they had self-cleaned, so we had quite a few saucepans in the cupboard or on the apricot tree. Soups and stews were okay because there was a lot of water in the ingredients, but steamed vegetables or rice were always burnt. Mum would start doing something else or go outside and get sidetracked and forget what was cooking, hence the blackened saucepans. People who came into the back garden would often comment, "Why do you keep your saucepans in a tree?"

Those who knew the situation asked, "Has your mum burnt another saucepan?"

It was a talking point and always gave us a laugh. Mum didn't seem to care one way or the other.

At Easter time, Mum made the most delicious hot cross buns, which she took great pride in and was well known for. She would prepare the dough on Good Friday Eve and in the morning it was ready to make into buns. They were full of dried fruit, and the smell of the sweet spicy dough as it cooked and cooled in the kitchen had us salivating at the kitchen table. At last, when they were cool enough to eat, we would run outside and over the road to tell our neighbours that Mum had made hot cross buns. The neighbours were over in a flash and soon sitting in the kitchen with a cup of tea and a bun. Mum enjoyed that little bit of notoriety and the company. We wanted her to make them every day but she wouldn't.

Christmas time was an even bigger event and the preparation began around October. There were three delicacies to be prepared for Christmas: fruit mince, plum pudding and the Christmas cake. Mum bought an enormous amount of dried fruit, nuts, eggs, butter, spices, a large piece of lard and a bottle of brandy. She had to order the lard from the butcher; it was a white solid thing that looked like copha. The bottle of brandy was only bought for the Christmas cooking.

The dried fruit was put into a large bowl and doused with brandy, then left to steep for a week. The fruit was then divided into three bowls to make three different things. One was made into fruit mince, so that meant there was an enormous amount of mincing and chopping and grating of apples and some suet. The mixture was put into glass jars, sealed and covered with a decorative Christmas fabric. Mum gave some of the jars away as Christmas gifts and for us she made delicious fruit mince tarts.

In the second bowl, the fruit for the puddings was mixed with suet, flour, spice and threepences, which had been saved up especially for Christmas. To make sure the coins were clean, they were always boiled for ten minutes. When the mixture was ready, it was divided and wrapped in calico, tied up with string and each one was steamed in a saucepan to cook. The puddings were then hung in the pantry to mature until Christmas Day.

Christmas cake was the thing I loved the most. As well as the dried fruit, it was full of cherries and almonds and the top was always decorated with blanched almonds in an attractive star arrangement. Mum would beat the butter and sugar on and off all day, gradually adding marmalade and eggs to the mixture. Lastly, the flour, spice and fruit were added. I liked to help so that I could eat some of the delicious concoction. The cakes took a long time to cook and the oven was on for twenty-four hours because there were usually at least four cakes. They were stored in airtight tins until Christmas time. My mother had the reputation of a Christmas cook extraordinaire, so the lucky people who received one of her creations had a special Christmas delicacy. I will never forget those delicious Christmas cakes. Mine are never quite as good.

Male Anatomy

When I was about thirteen, my brothers and I went with my mother for a two-week holiday at the Lord Mayor's Children's Camp at Portsea (I think that was the name of the camp). The mothers were mostly war widows or widows of husbands who had lost their lives as a result of war injuries. The boys and girls were housed in separate dormitories and the mothers shared rooms with other women and the smaller children. We had three good meals a day, served in a large informal dining room. It was all new to me and we made lots of friends. We were able to go down a steep staircase to the seashore every day but as it was during the autumn or winter, we kept away from the water.

One night, one of the older girls called Diane asked me to accompany her outside where she left me standing behind the girls' dormitory. A teenage boy called Ricky was standing there waiting for me. I was totally unaware of the plan that got me there. Apparently he fancied me but I had hardly noticed him until that meeting in the dark. He put his arms around me and kissed me on the lips. My first kiss. It was a pleasant surprise but I was a bit embarrassed when I saw him the next day. Diane tried to get me outside again but I refused to go. Who knows what could have happened to me if it had continued?

Diane said to me, "He really likes you."

"Oh, does he?"

"Yes, he likes you so much he has written your name on his thing."

"What thing?" I asked.

"You know, his thing."

"I don't know what thing you are talking about," I replied.

She came closer to me. "You know, his dick," she whispered.

I giggled a bit but I was not really sure what to think. It was all a bit too much for me. That was a good example of unwanted peer pressure. I did see Ricky again once in Melbourne and he called me a snob. That was the first time I had been called a snob, but certainly not the last.

About six years later, as a student nurse working in the Emergency Department at the Royal Melbourne Hospital, I saw one or two amazingly decorated penises, some tattooed with the name of a loved one. They reminded me of Ricky even though I never saw his penis. One day, what was thought to be a penis turned out to be salami that the man had stuffed down his jeans. He had been riding a motorbike and was involved in an accident in which he broke both his legs. We had to cut off his jeans and, as the jeans were cut up towards his groin, the salami (which had been secreted behind his zip) fell out. The senior nurse who I was assisting picked it up and without batting an eyelid popped it into a kidney dish and continued to cut off his jeans. The doctor present raised his eyebrows and continued inserting an intravenous line into the back of the man's hand. Later, in the privacy of the tearoom, it was mentioned and more senior people began to tell stories of all the weird and wonderful things they had seen.

Sometimes, when friends came over to my place, we would go to the telephone box around the corner to make phone calls just for something to do. Perhaps we were ringing other girls from school. I really can't remember. On one occasion, we were there making a phone call when a white car full of young boys pulled up. They started talking to us. One of them was a blue-eyed blonde who looked like Billy Idol. Billy Idol was not a thing then but in retrospect, that's what he looked like. He must have been eighteen because he was driving the car. He made it very clear that he liked me and I must admit I was attracted to him. His cousin went to the same school as me and on Monday morning she told me he was going to come to see me next weekend. He lived somewhere in the country and he drove all the way down to Melbourne to see me. Once again, he was more advanced in the boyfriend/girlfriend thing than I was and after a few visits, he began to worry me. He always wanted me to lie down next to him and, although it was a nice thing to do, it frightened me when he said, "Do you realise there is only a small piece of cloth between your body and mine? Wouldn't it be nice if there was nothing between our skin?"

Something moved and I got up and went inside to find Mum. I didn't tell her about him. He soon stopped coming to see me when I wouldn't spend time alone with him.

I'm making it sound like I was not normal, but these things all happened when I was very young and naive. However, I did grow up and embrace the whole male/female thing with gusto.

James, my first real boyfriend, the pianist, could play Flight of the Bumble Bee (which I loved) and various other difficult pieces. One night when he came to see me, my brothers and I were in the living room. I was standing up at the piano trying to play Für Elise which I thought would impress James. He came and stood very close to me. I felt something firm against my thigh. Turning around, I looked down and from the top of his low-waisted jeans, a pink thing with what looked like an eye on the top was peering at me. Yes, I had brothers, but this was different and I was so shocked. Realising what it was, I hurried out of the living room and into the kitchen where I sat in front of the stove, put my feet in the oven door and became engrossed in a book. Another time, he took me to a car show at the Exhibition Building. It was very crowded and we walked around hand-in-hand like any boyfriend and girlfriend. We were crushed up at a display of some sort when I accidentally let go of his hand. Knowing he was behind me, I put my hand out to grab his but I grabbed his genitals instead. I was instantly aware of a response in my hand. Once again, I was shocked and embarrassed. I had not known about that anatomical reaction. He didn't say anything so I didn't either. I am pleased to say that these things became clear to me as normal anatomical reactions, but it would have been better had I been prepared. I think … or would it?

Gaffney Street

When I was in Year Seven, we had a phone call from Janice's mother asking if I could stay for a few weeks over the summer holidays to keep Janice company while her parents were at work. Mum seemed to think it would be okay, so we went on the train to Coburg station where we met Janice and her mum. Mum went straight back home on the train and I went in a neighbour's car to Janice's place. Janice's parents both worked at the Queen Victoria Market and left early in the morning so we were on our own more than half the time. At night, I slept in the bedroom with Janice and her beautiful older sister Marion. I had to sleep on the floor on a skinny camp mattress which was so thin I might as well have been sleeping on the carpet. After a few nights, I asked Janice if we could swap beds but she refused, so I continued to try to get a good night's sleep on the floor. During the day we didn't do much, and it became very boring and Janice became very bossy towards me. She was always telling me what to do or criticising me for the smallest things. I am the type of person who will take quite a bit until it becomes too much and then I let fly. This is what happened after ten days, so I just let her know that I was fed up with her bossiness and the sleeping arrangement. I packed my enormous suitcase and set off down the hill towards Pascoe Vale Railway Station. It was about forty degrees and I didn't have any money for a train ticket, but I didn't care. I couldn't stand it any longer. Luckily, I didn't get apprehended on the train for not having a ticket. I arrived home and told Mum why I had come home before the prearranged time. I didn't hear anything from Janice for about six years, not until I met her by accident in the city when she was working in a bank and I was working at Myer. Our friendship was reignited for the third time.

More School

I went to an all-girls' school and it was a pretty good school really. The teachers were mostly nice, and quite motherly and supportive. All except one; a maths teacher called Mrs Popov. I think she had migrated to Australia from Hungary after World War II. I was scared to death of her and I didn't learn much because she was so awful. She yelled at the top of her voice and whacked the front desk with a large ruler, which made everyone jump in fright. Whatever maths I knew before Mrs Popov came along was as far as I went. I got really nervous when a maths class was coming up and that was about four times a week. She would put a problem on the board and always asked someone like me to get up and solve it. I could not think past the simplest problems and would end up just staring at the board in embarrassment. Then she would call up a more competent girl to complete the maths problem and make me look even sillier. At the end-of-year maths exam, I received 32%—my first failure at secondary school. When I applied to be a nurse, this 32% was pointed out as a problem that I would have to overcome if I wanted to be accepted. I had to sit a maths exam so I got tutoring from my older brother and passed the exam easily. The other teachers (as I remember them) were great, especially as we got older. Miss Barrow, an art teacher, always complimented me on my painting and through her teaching in art history and appreciation, she initiated my love of art, especially French and Australian impressionists. I still love these paintings more than any others to this day.

I got very excited during a science lesson when the whole class had just completed the dissection of a lab rat each. Something compelled me to whistle out loud. Miss Dawson stopped mid-sentence and declared, "Who whistled?"

No one answered.

"Who whistled?" she repeated.

No reply.

"I will repeat this one more time and then everything will change." Silence.

"Well, we will all sit here until four o'clock unless someone tells me who it was."

My heart sank. I knew I couldn't be responsible for the whole grade being kept in so I had to put up my hand and confess to the dreadful transgression. Therefore, I was the only one who was kept in till four o'clock writing lines: 'I must not whistle in class.'

Miss Bradford was a music teacher who drove a funny little car called a Goggomobil. She gave us music lessons in the school hall so she could play the piano for us. She also encouraged us to sing and asked me to join the choir, which I did. One day, someone brought a lipstick to school and during the music lesson it was passed to me, daring me to put some on. I did. Miss Bradford spotted it immediately (it was bright pink).

"Get out," she yelled at me. "How dare you! Remove it and go to see Miss Daniels."

I slunk off to the toilets to remove the lipstick with toilet paper and then I reported to the Headmistress for my punishment. I had to stay after school for half an hour and write one hundred times: 'school girls do not wear lipstick at school'. I certainly didn't wear lipstick at school again.

Miss Bradford's car, the Goggomobil, made a lot of noise and we always knew when she was arriving at school because of the racket. I could hardly believe my ears when, at home one Saturday, I heard the familiar sound of Miss Bradford's Goggomobil driving down our street. She had moved into rooms down the road from us in a beautiful Edwardian timber house. The owner was one of the spinsters who had lost her fiancé during the war. The noise the Goggomobil made was obviously due to a need for mechanical attention, which it did not get. One morning it would not start and it remained parked out in the street until someone towed it away to be repaired. When the car was returned to her, it made no sound at all. I was disappointed that I couldn't hear her coming and going because I was curious to see if she had a boyfriend. One day, my curiosity was satisfied when I saw her sitting in her car with a man. All the girls at school begged me for the story the following week, so I had to elaborate and added that there was a lot of kissing and cuddling in broad daylight. The poor woman would not have been impressed with my ridiculous spying and exaggerated story telling.

One of my friends at secondary school was Marina, an attractive Italian girl who was much more physically mature than me. She wore tight knitwear and tailored slacks. I had a pair of Blackwatch tartan slacks which I wore with a long, baggy yellow cardigan. Not really fashionable, but I didn't have much choice. On the way to the local picture theatre on a Saturday afternoon, two older boys approached us. One of these boys was very good-looking and popular with lots of girls. He looked Marina up and down and said, "I'd like to fuck you."

Marina was thrilled that he was taking an interest in her and got all giggly and silly. The next Monday at school, she wrote a letter to the boy and passed it to me to read. The letter read:

Dear John
When you said you would like to fuck me did you mean it?

The teacher saw the letter being passed back to Marina and asked to see the note. We were both in big trouble and were called to the Headmistress's office separately. Miss Daniels asked me if I had written the note and I said no. (It was obvious I had not written it just by looking at our different handwriting.) Marina's parents were called to the school and chose to believe their daughter who denied writing the note. She was forbidden to speak to the girl who wore the stupid long yellow cardigan and whenever I saw her, she would put her nose in the air and ignore me. I suppose you can't blame her parents for wanting to believe their daughter would not write such a note. I told Mum, who was horrified to hear that I had been friends with a girl who would write the word 'fuck'.

Another friend at school was Angela Brown, a very plain-looking girl actually. A very, very plain girl, but she was lots of fun. She had the frizziest hair I have ever seen, she was overweight, had freckles, wore thick glasses and had dreadful acne on her face. She was witty and good at maths (unlike me). She came to my place after school sometimes and we did our homework together. She tried to help me with maths. One day, we went to her place and I met her mother for the first time. Angela was a dead ringer for her mother except her mother had grey hair and no acne. She wasn't a very nice mother because she looked at me and began to berate Angela for not having a clear complexion like mine, for not having long straight hair and for not being pretty. I couldn't believe what I was hearing. It was awful, but Angela just ignored what her mother said and took me to the kitchen to make us a toasted ham and cheese sandwich and a milkshake each.

The Beatles

In 1964, the Beatles came to Melbourne. The father of one of my friends bought tickets for a few of us to go to the concert. A day or two before the concert we went to see them when they arrived at Essendon Airport. There were quite a lot of people waiting. Unfortunately after the Beatles walked off the aeroplane and onto the tarmac they were quickly put into a car and driven away. We ran after the car and as it slowed down a bit to pass through a gate, I put my hands on the car and I could see them grinning at us from the interior. The car took off and ran over my foot but that did not stop me. I began to run after the car until my suspender belt broke and my stockings fell down into my boots. The car disappeared down the road towards the city.

Several days later, we went to the concert at Festival Hall. It was extremely noisy and full of excited teenagers. I can't remember which band played before the Beatles and I don't think I could hear them anyway. When the Beatles finally came on stage the noise from the audience was amazingly loud—deafening actually. Everybody was screaming at the top of their lungs. Even me. I don't know why, and I certainly hadn't intended to scream, but I screamed and jumped about just like all the others around me. I could see the four mop-topped boys singing away and playing their guitars, but I couldn't hear anything except overexcited teenagers screeching at the top of their lungs. Mass hysteria they said. My throat was sore for days afterwards. Everyone had a favourite Beatle. Mine was George Harrison.

Peeping Tom

Two doors up the hill from us lived a family with four boys and a girl. The boys were a highly mischievous group, always up to some sort of bad behaviour. Their mother always looked stressed and rarely smiled. Once, one of these boys lit a firecracker and put it into my brother's pocket. My brother had a couple of firecrackers already in his pocket and they all exploded. He sustained a very nasty burn on his upper thigh and still has the scar.

One night, I was in the bathroom getting ready to have a shower when I thought I heard something at the window. Looking out, I couldn't see anything because it was too dark. The next time I heard the noise, I was getting ready to shower. I quickly turned out the light and hurried to the window. There, perched up on top of the fence, was one of those boys staring in the window. We didn't have a blind on the window because it was very high up, but if someone climbed onto the top of the fence everything in the bathroom could be seen, such as me having a shower or bath. Mum put a blind up next day.

Losing My Religion

When I decided to become a nurse, I had no idea what that meant. I imagined I would wear a uniform and that it would most likely be white. I also supposed that I would take the odd temperature or two. Basically, I had no idea what it was all about. I suspect that if we young school leavers had known what we were in for, we would have run a mile. We were fitted out with six blue-striped dresses and twelve starched white aprons and were requested to buy a pair of sensible black shoes, four pairs of grey stockings, a packet of white bobby pins and white-headed sewing pins.

The first night of our nurses' training we gathered at a beautiful old house in Toorak called Trawalla, which is where we lived for six weeks of Preliminary Training School (PTS). Our uniforms were waiting for us, along with a red woollen cape and a little white book of the New Testament. One brave girl declined the New Testament stating that she was an atheist, but she was persuaded to accept it anyway because it had been inscribed with her name. Another also declined the little book because she was Jewish. I was already learning about the big wide world outside of Moonee Ponds.

We were instructed on how to wear our uniforms and how to keep the silly little caps on our heads. Take one white tissue, fold it into a small square, pin this square to the top of your head with white bobby pins, pop the cap onto your head and, with two sewing pins, secure the cap to the tissue. Mastering the cap was a real accomplishment. Quite a few girls pricked their heads and we all giggled a lot because we thought we looked weird or because we were excited.

We spent six weeks in PTS before being let loose onto the ward, under the guidance of a senior nurse. It was an enormous learning curve for all of us and some of the things we encountered were barely mentioned in PTS, if at all. The sisters in charge of the wards were strict and unapproachable. Some of them were not very nice and were renowned for giving a new nurse a difficult duty on their first day. Mine was to give an enema to an elderly spinster woman who was very reluctant to expose her buttocks to me.

"You're just a child, you shouldn't be doing such things. Where's the doctor?" she said to me.

Fortunately, one of the tutor sisters came to give me a hand, which taught me that no matter how senior the nurse is, if the patient doesn't want a tube stuck up her posterior, she will fight it. And she did fight. The tutor sister got poo on her white dress and I didn't. Who ever heard of a doctor giving an enema? Not me. I survived the first day and continued to be surprised almost every day, usually not pleasantly. I had another encounter with the enema tube where the patient did not want to co-operate. An elderly Scottish man with an incomprehensible accent yelled at the top of his voice, "Get that bloody thing out of my arse and leave me alone, I'll shit when I'm ready."

I left him alone.

I worked in the Casualty department, now called Emergency, for a few months. On Saturday nights I spent many hours in the theatre assisting sixth-year medical students suturing lacerations and cuts sustained on the streets of Melbourne. On cold winter nights it was common for the waiting room seats to be occupied by sad homeless men who were tolerated by the sister in charge. We students would give them jam sandwiches which we made at our supper time and secretly carried back to them under our red nurse's capes. The sister in charge of the department did not encourage us in feeding them.

If any of these people had to be admitted for treatment the first thing we were required to do was give them a bath, not an easy thing to do in some cases, but they loved the warm bed and three meals a day.

I had nightmares from day one about a poor old dear who had been on a respirator for some time. During the day, we were trying tried to encourage her to breathe on her own so the tracheotomy orifice was partly plugged with a small cork. The woman was very thin and relatively toothless, with long white hair. In my dream she was a witch, but by day she was a very sick old lady nearing death.

In the bed next to her was a dear old Italian woman called Mrs Italiano, who was suffering from an abdominal mass, probable cancer, but it was discovered too late and there was no treatment to save her, just analgesics for her pain. Being a good Catholic she prayed frequently using her rosary beads and the priest visited her daily. I think I probably said a prayer for her, as I still had a tiny belief in God. She really took a liking to me, and me to her. I was embarrassed because she called me 'Sister', which I certainly was not, and I thought I would get into trouble if one of the sisters heard. Mrs Italiano was discharged and taken home by her lovely family, only to return one evening about 9pm. She was moaning and obviously in a lot of pain and bleeding from her rectum. I was called in to help clean her up and make her comfortable, but as soon as we cleaned her, the blood gushed out of her and she began to fade right in front of our eyes. At first it was old blood called melena but it soon became fresh blood. After she was seen by the doctor (who said there was nothing he could do), the sister I was working with decided to let her lie still and called her family to be with her as she died. This was my first experience with death. As a nurse, it horrified me. What about all the praying? What about all the words the priest said directly to God? And why did her death have to be so traumatic? I cried along with her family. I thought God could perform miracles and at least be kind to his devotees when they died. Of course, there was always my father's death at the back of my mind, which continued to haunt me.

There were many other instances that affected my religious beliefs, but the one that really put a cap on it for me was little Robby Bathhouse.

At the end of our second year of nursing we went to the Royal Children's Hospital for three months to gain some paediatric experience. I was placed in the neurological ward, and most days I worked in 'Section One' where seriously ill children were cared for. One of these was dear little Robby. Till the day I die I will never forget this very sick, darling little boy who was suffering from muscular dystrophy. He was four years old and his mother never came to see him. He was dying, he couldn't move, he couldn't feed himself, he was back in nappies and he cried for his mother constantly. Sometimes he called me Mummy and that broke my heart. One day I said to one of the nurses from St Vincent's, "Doesn't this make you doubt your belief in God?"

She replied, "No, it makes me more holy."

I don't understand that and I don't want to understand such a selfish and ridiculous attitude. This conversation took place just after we had wheeled the bed into the bathroom to bathe a limp, paralysed Robby who was, as usual, crying for his mother.

In the bed opposite Robby was a ten-year-old boy called John who had an inoperable brain tumour. His mother spent all day with him and sometimes, if John was asleep, she would sit with Robby, hold his hand and read to him. The sister in charge of the ward did contact Robby's mother, more than once, but I never saw her visit him. He died in his sleep one night; so did John.

Life is so sad and so unfair sometimes. God or nature, whatever you want to call it: there is no rhyme or reason to much of what happens.

So that's where my atheism came from, and no one will change my mind.

Transport and Tossers
Or Why I Stopped Using Public Transport

Car ownership was not as common as it is today so most people used public transport. We were fortunate to have both train and tram lines near where we lived: the Moonee Ponds Railway Station, and further up Puckle Street was the tramline into the city.

I don't remember how old I was the first time I was confronted by a man staring at me as he fished around in his pocket trying to find something. At least, that's what I thought was happening. The next time I saw a man doing the same thing he actually found what he was looking for, and took it out to show me. I was not impressed. Once, as I sat in a very crowded train, a man stood in front of me with his fly open and I suppose he was getting some pleasure from my closeness and embarrassment at having to view his hairy pubic area. Why didn't I say something? I suppose it was my young age and also I wondered if it was accidental.

Walking up to Puckle Street one time wearing a pair of pedal-pushers that I had just finished sewing, a man said to me, "That's a nice little c∗∗∗ you have there love."

I was twelve. I turned and went home.

As I was walking home from the train one evening, a man who

had been following closely behind me tried to grab me, but I yelled and ran home. I saw him several days later with his wife and children.

There were several incidents on a crowded tram where a man grabbed my breast from behind. He got an elbow in the ribs. The next time this happened I yelled out, "Keep your hands to yourself," and gave him a backwards kick in the shin. He got off at the next stop and hurried away from the tram tracks. Another time, a man sat opposite me, then next to me, on the train. I moved and he moved next to me. I moved again and he did the same, even though the train was virtually empty. Then there was the young guy who waggled his penis at me as we passed each other under the subway in Moonee Ponds in broad daylight. I yelled at him and chased him with my umbrella. Coming home from the city one evening on an almost empty train, I was pestered by a man who really wanted to sit near me. There were plenty of seats but he was determined to be close to me. Moving did not deter him. He kept a newspaper in front of him hiding his moving hand and he was muttering quietly to himself. I was really scared of him and hoped he would get off before me. He got off at my stop and there wasn't a railway employee in sight. A young man who had also alighted from the train was walking along the platform towards me. I didn't know him but I asked him if he would walk with me at least to my street, which he did. That was the last time I went on public transport at night on my own. It is not new that women are not safe on their own in some circumstances, but it is extremely annoying and very unfair because it stops us from feeling safe and doing the things we have every right to do.

My Future

In 1965, the Rolling Stones came to Melbourne and played at the Palais Theatre in St Kilda. I went with my friend Janice who had been given tickets. It was a Friday night in January and we caught a tram from the city. I don't remember much about the concert except that Mick Jagger had an amazing amount of energy. He pranced up and down on the stage in front of the curtain while he sang and played his guitar. It was fun but not as exciting or as noisy as the Beatles concert. After the concert, we went into the city to a disco called Downbeat, which was in a lane off Lonsdale Street. A live band was playing, I can't remember which one, but it was loud and the lights were dim and there were boys eyeing girls and girls eyeing boys—nothing new. My friend Janice liked a certain type of boy and she looked at one and made a comment about him. I looked at him and the next thing I knew he was asking me to dance. I found out later that they were two boys who didn't know each other and one had said to the other, "Do you want to ask those girls to dance?"

They approached us and one boy got to Janice first and the other boy asked me. Apparently, they were both heading for Janice (blonde always preferred.)

I continued to go out with this boy, who was a little younger than me, for six years. We were married in April 1971 and as I write, we have just had our 50th wedding anniversary.

Epilogue

As I wrote in my Introduction, what I have written is basically true. I have altered some names and embellished a little here and there. It was not a fun time, it was not a happy childhood, but it is mine and it has influenced me and made me who I am.

I enjoyed the sixties, which were great years: the job availabilities, the independence, the new educational opportunities, the Pill, the music, the political awareness and freedom of expression. Women were finally being heard (a little) and were standing up and speaking for themselves and other women.

I am proud to say that I took part in the anti-Vietnam protests and the biggest demonstration, in which thousands of us sat down in the centre of Bourke Street. I also demonstrated against the unfair conscription of young men into the army to fight in Vietnam after our Prime Minister, Harold Holt, said "All the way with LBJ".

I have made some friends and lost some friends, I have cared for people and saved some lives. I have been married to the same man for more than fifty years and I have raised four children of whom I am very proud. I have loved and been loved in return.

I have seen some of the most famous Australian and international entertainers, I have read many books and I have travelled quite a lot. I have viewed an amazing number of well-known paintings in galleries in Australia and Europe and I have stood in some magnificent old buildings, castles and ancient ruins.

I love the simple things in life, specifically nature and in particular animals, the mountains and the sky, and because of these things I consider myself a very fortunate woman.

My relationship with my mother was never very good or close. I can only remember her complimenting me on two occasions, the first on the day I was married. She said to me, "You look nice, dear."

She just did not seem to understand me and sometimes I think she didn't like me very much as we were so different. I know I sometimes spoke impulsively and said things without thinking, and this caused quite a lot of difficulty between us. We disagreed about her way of dealing with a difficult situation—she would act quickly and move on, not wanting to deal with the situation properly or with any consideration. She would either do what had been done to her, or what she thought was the best way to deal with something, then she would put it out of her mind. I am thinking of the way she dealt with the kittens and also my sneaking off to see my boyfriend instead of going to my piano lesson. I have forgiven her for the things she did to me, the things that really hurt me and seemed to be really silly and sometimes cruel.

When she was very old, she came to live with me and I looked after her for about six years. As she aged, she mellowed, and I think she saw me differently and realised I was not so bad after all. Her life had been hard and she did what she thought was right and that's that.

As I got older, I thought about her life and I began to understand my mother and to feel very sorry for her. Born in 1907 into a very strict family, she lived through World Wars I and II, the Great Depression, being widowed after only ten years of marriage and having to bring up four young children on her own. She was a woman who never reached her full potential but because she was well educated and quite clever, I think it would have been a different story for her today.

THE AUTHOR

Margaret Lygnos lives with her husband in regional Victoria. Her previous books are Poppy and Group Therapy. All three titles are available online.